You Too Can Be AN INTELLIGENT INVESTOR

An A to Z Guide to Investing in Stock Markets, Real Estate, Mutual Funds, Commodities and Currency

You Too Can Be AN INTELLIGENT INVESTOR

An **A to Z** Guide to
Investing in Stock Markets, Real Estate, Mutual Funds, Commodities and Currency

MAHESH CHANDRA KAUSHIK
SEBI Registered & NISM Certified Stock Market Research Analyst

PRABHAT
PRAKASHAN

No part of this publication can be reproduced, stored in a retrieval system or transmitted in any form or by any means, electronic, mechanical, photocopying, recording or otherwise, without prior permission of the author. Rights of this book are with the author.

Published by
PRABHAT PRAKASHAN PVT. LTD.
4/19 Asaf Ali Road,
New Delhi-110 002 (INDIA)
e-mail: prabhatbooks@gmail.com

ISBN 978-93-5521-299-3
YOU TOO CAN BE AN INTELLIGENT INVESTOR
by Mahesh Chandra Kaushik

© Reserved

Edition
2025

Price
₹ 350 (Rupees Three Hundred Fifty Only)

Printed at
R-Tech Offset Printers, Delhi

Introduction

A smart and intelligent investor must always analyse the long-term growth potential of a company and the efficiency of its management before making an investment.

A smart investor should diversify his investments as diversification can save you from possible future losses. A smart investor never seeks irrational profits but focuses on safe, stable and regular returns.

Safe and regular returns are of utmost importance. Those who are my regular followers must have seen my video in which I have said that if you book a profit of only ₹ 500 in a trade, then your profit will be ₹ 1 crore by undertaking 20,000 such trades. Therefore, rather than being greedy and dreaming of earning ₹ 1 crore from a single trade, it is better to earn ₹ 500 each from 20,000 small trades and reach ₹ 1 crore.

If you want to become a smart and intelligent investor, then rely on your own research and completely ignore the rumours and tips circulating in the market. You should never think that the general public cannot earn money from the market. Although there are good and bad performers in the stock market there is no such thing as a truly perfect stock. The stock price is good at which its valuation is low-priced and it has the potential for future growth.

You should act like an investor in the stock market and not a speculator. In the stock market, it is necessary to invest your capital by dividing it into small parts so that you never lose all your money.

Always remember my advice – "Your first priority in the stock market should be safety and your second priority should be to make consistent profits."

In this world, people earn money in four ways:

1. By working as employees: This category includes company employees, government employees, labourers, etc. Here, you have to invest most of your time and labour. The better you plan your time and labour, the more your income will be.
2. As shopkeepers and professionals: Shopkeepers, doctors, lawyers, etc. fall into this category. They also have to actively plan their time and effort.
3. As a businessman or company owner: In this category of investment, the company owner is required to be active. He may take a vacation for some time, but he cannot earn passive income for long.
4. As an investor: This category of income is completely passive income. Here, your money works for you. You can spend your time having fun and doing things that interest you. People in this category are really rich because they have both money and time.

So, if you fall into the first three categories mentioned above, then you must think about earning income as an investor. Becoming an investor increases your chances of getting rich.

But for this, you will need to work hard in the right direction. You have to develop the ability to identify which stock is overpriced and which stock is undervalued because most of the small investors buy overpriced shares by watching others and later regret losing their money.

I will explain this to you through a practical example. The stock of a big steel company was around ₹ 300 for the last 2 or 3 years. Then suddenly there was a rise in its prices and within 1 year its share increased by 5 times to ₹ 1,500. Once, around that time, I went to the market. My shopkeeper told me happily that the company was giving tremendous returns, so yesterday he had invested two lakhs at the rate of ₹ 1,584. I then asked him when the same share cost around ₹ 300 for two years, why he had not bought it and why he bought it only for ₹ 1,584. The shopkeeper panicked at my question and said with concern, "Yes sir, this is true. What should I do now? Should I sell it tomorrow?"

I could not give him an answer because the price of that share could have risen even more. But this is not the hallmark of a smart investor. The wise investor buys undervalued shares and sells overpriced shares.

Therefore, instead of buying shares by guessing whether the market will rise or fall, you will have to learn to calculate the valuation of the stock and buy and sell shares on the basis of whether the stock is low-priced or expensive.

If you buy shares based on the assumption of whether the market will rise or fall, then instead of becoming an investor you become a speculator who earns for operators and broker companies but loses money himself.

The stock market is volatile and investors want to take advantage of these fluctuations. For this reason, when the market rises, they buy shares at high prices in the hope that the market will rise even more, and when the market starts falling, they sell the shares at a very low rate based on the concept of stop loss. But by doing so, they convert themselves into speculators instead of an investor.

Both rise and fall in the stock market take place as inevitable and optional. These ups and downs or fluctuations in the stock market are a sign of the beauty of the market. That's why the great investor Graham said, "Do not sell a stock because it is falling and do not buy a stock because it is rising."

However, this statement does not mean that you have to buy every falling stock and sell every rising stock. Basically, your work should be based more on quality rather than price.

In fact, the stock market is not a casino. It is a market that provides you with opportunities to earn additional income, where if you act wisely, you will buy shares from pessimists and sell shares to optimists and earn enough money to meet your needs.

New readers will be glad to know that the book you are reading is my seventh book on investment and the last 6 books were bestsellers owing to the support and love of the readers. In this seventh book, based on my 17 years of stock market experience and from the present-day perspective, I have offered you not only the information about the latest methods but in addition to the stock market, I have also made an attempt to explain all aspects of investment like mutual funds, commodity, currency, real estate, and algo trading as well.

I am also grateful to my wife Mrs. Seema Kaushik, who has always encouraged my new investment ideas and also unhesitatingly offered the hard-earned money from her YouTube channel 'Seema Ki Rasoi' to invest according to my new inventions in the stock market. Lastly, I am grateful to my Sadguru Dev Shree Shri 1008 Satyanarayanji Falahari Baba, with whose blessings God made me a medium for completing this task of guiding you.

If you get bored while reading the initial chapters of the book or you feel that all these are elementary-level things and you already know them, even then read the book continuously. The next chapters of the book contain the following special information, which you will not find in any other publication on investment:

1. Super Breakout Method for Intraday
2. Complete System of Trading on Margin without Paying Interest
3. 1-5 Methods to Get Regular Monthly Income from NiftyBees
4. Flow Method of Investing in Commodities Like Gold and Silver
5. Calendar Spread Method of Currency Trading

So, don't read this book half-heartedly. I request you to read it at least twice and make notes of the necessary facts. I can convinced that my years of hard work will pay off and with the help of the book, you will definitely achieve financial prosperity. You can also e-mail me at mahesh2073@yahoo.com. I do not give my mobile number as I have close to 2 lakh followers because how can 2 lakh people be guided on the mobile? But I try my best to answer the e-mails of as many readers as possible.

Yours sincerely,

–Mahesh Chandra Kaushik
Certified Registered Research Analyst
Assistant Revenue Accounts Officer
Collector Office, Sirohi
Rajasthan – 307022

Contents

1
Introduction to the Stock Market

"There are two main rules of the stock market – rule number one, never lose your money, and rule number two, never forget rule number one."

– ***Warren Buffett***

At present, trading in stock markets has become completely digital rather than physical. A stock market is a platform where a shareholder sells his shares and a person willing to buy shares buys them. Thus, the stock market provides a digital platform to both the buyer and seller, where both can undertake transactions easily.

News related to a specific sector or share in the stock markets can affect all the stocks in that sector or a share related to it, whereby money can be earned by taking advantage of the shares of that sector. In this book, you will be given complete information about the basic knowledge of the stock market as well as how to take advantage of the movement.

The Initial Requirement for Share Trading: In the past, for share trading, people used to approach their local sub-broker and place orders to buy and sell shares. Just like you buy goods by visiting a shop now, in the same way, at that time, to buy or sell shares you had to go to the local sub-broker and place an order. Gradually, with the development of the telephone, people called their brokers and placed orders to buy and sell shares. Then came the age of computers. The 'business terminal software' was used for this task, which is still in use.

After that, brokerage companies launched their online trading platforms and after the arrival of mobiles, stock trading took place on mobile apps. Nowadays almost all major brokerage companies have mobile apps. Therefore, to start trading in shares, the first initial requirement is to have a smartphone or an Android mobile, which everyone has nowadyas.

How Shares are Bought and Sold: This book has been written in the beginning with basics keeping in mind the absolutely unaware investor. That's why you need to understand how shares are bought and sold through mobile apps, etc. When you place an order with your broker to buy a share from your trading account, you have two options:

1. Buying shares at the limit price
2. Buying shares at market price

That means, if you decide that you do not want to buy shares over a particular price, then you will ask for the limit price and if you want the shares to be bought for you at any price prevalent in the market, then you will place the order at the market price.

For example, you place an order to buy 100 shares of the State Bank of India at a price of ₹ 440 and if you buy them for shareholding, then you should have a sufficient amount in your account (for intraday you can buy more shares with less amount, which will be explained to you later). Similarly, if another investor places an order to sell 100 shares at a price of 440, then there should be enough shares in his account.

Now your orders are sent to the stock exchange. The deal is executed when the limit price of the orders of both those who wish to buy, hold and sell the stock match. The process of transferring the seller's Demat account to the stock buyer's Demat account is initiated by the exchange. Similarly, the process of transferring the amount to the seller from the buyer's bank account or from money deposited with the broker begins.

The above stock and cash transfer take two days, which is called the 'settlement cycle'. It is also colloquially called T+2 settlement. Presently the process of reducing the settlement time from 2 days to 1 day is in progress. It is being implemented in a phased manner.

In your business strategy, always calculate profits with the annual growth rate-

If you have read my book Abdul Share Bazar Mein Zero Se Hero Kaise Bane? which was written as a novel, then you will be familiar with a character named Ghisu Bhai, who would buy a share for ₹ 100 and sell it for not less than ₹ 120. Ghisu Bhai would sell a share only after making at least 20 percent profit even if he had to hold it for 5 years. This method of profit calculation is known as absolute return, in which—

Share purchase price = ₹ 100

Selling price of the share = ₹ 120

Profit = ₹ (120-100) = ₹ 20

Profit percentage = (20/100) x 100 = 20 percent

But this is not the correct method of profit calculation as the time factor is not taken into consideration. If this 20 percent profit is made in a few months or 1 to 2 years, then this profit is an attractive profit or good profit. But if you have earned the same profit over a period of 4 years, then is it attractive? No, it is not attractive at all because by earning ₹ 20 rupees against ₹ 100 in 4 years, Ghisu Bhai has earned less than 4 percent per annum.

Contrary to this absolute return, if you calculate the profit with the Annual Growth Rate (CAGR), then you can take out the annual growth tax on your investment. This is called Compound Annual Growth Rate (CAGR), which is more accurate. In the above example, if Ghisu Bhai made 120 with 100 in 5 years, then its CAGR is 3.71 percent, which is less than the interest earned on the savings account.

How to Calculate CAGR: You don't need to use elaborate maths formula and calculations nowadays to calculate the annual growth rate. You can just type 'Online CAGR Calculator' in Google and easily calculate CAGR with the help of online calculators and know whether the return from your investment strategy is more than bank interest rate etc. and attractive or not.

Types of Investors and Business Styles: On the basis of their business style, there are three types of investors:

1. **Swing Investors or Short-Term Investors:** These investors try to make profits from the fluctuations in the prices of the shares and their investments can be for a few days, a few weeks, or a few months.
2. **Growth Investor or Long-Term Investor:** These investors invest for a period ranging from a few years to several decades.
3. **Value Investor:** This most sensible class of investors, i.e. Value Investor, knows that he has to buy blue-chip shares of reputable companies in the stock market two or three times a year at cheap prices, as a result of which they get excellent profit opportunities in the future. I have an SRNTV method i.e. 'Share Genius Ratio of Nifty Technical Valuation' to find out the exact timing of stocks that are available at cheap prices in the stock market. You can watch my YouTube video about it by searching my YouTube video or reading the description in my book How to Get Financial Freedom with the Miracle of SIP. In short, in this method, the current market price of a share/index is divided by its 124 DMA and if this quotient is less than 0.96, then the value of the share

is fair. If you start SIP in a stock or ETF after the price/124 day moving average is below 096, then such SIP gives maximum profit. Conversely, if the price/124 day average crosses 1.12, then it is the right time to start profit booking. I had originally discovered the SRNTV method for Nifty. But from the e-mails of my followers, I learnt that the followers were also making lucrative profits by using it to do SIP in blue-chip stocks included in the Nifty 50.

So, this was a short description of the Indian stock market. However, to get started, you will first need to open a Demat account through a broker. The process of opening a Demat account will be described further.

Common Mistakes in the Stock Market and How to Avoid Them: Working in the stock market is very exciting. In this adventure, when new investors make their first profit, they start thinking that they have got a magic wand and that they are going to get rich soon. Mistakes start with this thought. New investors make many mistakes in a hurry to get rich, which eventually turn into losses. Then they make more mistakes in the process of making up for the losses and owing to continuous losses, they eventually lose interest in the stock market thinking that their decision to enter the stock market was wrong and that they can never make a profit from it.

Now I will describe those mistakes to you so that you can see whether you are committing these mistakes intentionally or unintentionally.

1. **Don't Rush to Get Rich:** Most of the new investors enter the stock market with the dream of making millions in a few months. If you also wish to become a millionaire in a few days, then the chances of this happening are very less. All the great investors or millionaires who have become millionaires in the history of the stock market have become millionaires by slowly growing through the 'Power of Compounding'.

2. **You Must Gain Knowledge of the Stock Market:** New investors at the beginner level imitate other investors in the market. But they do not understand the market. Such investors either buy very expensive stocks or walk away with a small profit before they understand it. Therefore, buying and selling shares only on the basis of your limited knowledge or imitation causes many mistakes. So, first, gather knowledge by reading books by the stalwarts of this field or listening to successful investors on YouTube. (There are also several channels on YouTube run by ignorant people. So, don't watch a channel based only on the number of subscribers, rather check whether the person giving information on the channel is SEBI registered and an NISM certified research analyst and whether he is counted among the big investors and advisors in the stock market.) You can also take the stock market courses on your own from NISM (National Institute of Stock Market). With respect to online courses, you can join very high-level courses in Hindi and English medium for free on the Varsity website or the Varsity app. Varsity is an online learning course provided by a broker named Zerodha. Right now, the course is available on the app only in English. But on the website, it is available in both Hindi and English. Its special feature is that it is free and it also provides certificates.

3. **Make Proper Use of the Concept of Stop-Loss:** If you buy shares for a very limited time based on some rumour or news, then keep a certain percentage in your mind. This is called stop loss. It means that I will not incur more loss than this and if there is this much loss, then I will collect my remaining money. However, I am not a supporter of the concept of stop-loss as this option is only for intraday traders and future traders working on short-term or leverage and not for investors who invest their own money in good blue-chip companies. Next, I will tell you about those methods, by

which you can calculate effective averaging when the stock falls in a long-term investment instead of a stop loss.

4. **Exposure or Leverage:** Exposure or leverage is a double-edged sword. My honest advice to you is that if you are a new investor, do not use exposure or leverage. Basically, leverage or exposure means creating a position that is bigger than your potential (capability). New stock traders (they cannot be called investors) want to make more profit by investing less money. Therefore, they use exposure or leverage. For example your broker gives you the facility that you can buy 50,000 shares by investing 10,000 in intraday. New investors are happy with this facility as they think that taking leverage in intraday will increase their profits. Suppose you buy 50,000 shares and they increase by 2 percent, which is 2 percent of 50,000 which means a total profit of ₹ 1000. In this way, new investors think that they invested 10,000 and earned 1000, i.e. they got 10 percent profit. Therefore, they think that by using leverage, they make a profit of 10 percent if the share increases by 2 percent, i.e. their profit can increase 5 times.

But remember one thing clearly that it can also increase the loss just like profit. This increased loss can not only wipe out your business capital but can also put you in a debt.

In fact, when there is a big fall in the market, the shares can fall by 10 to 20 percent in a single day. Suppose someone's trading capital is 10,000 and he takes an exposure of 50,000 in intraday taking advantage of leverage and unfortunately, the stock falls up to 20 percent. So, in a single day, his entire capital can be wiped out due to 20 percent loss = 10,000 on 50,000. To lure small investors with exposure or leverage, they are taught the concept of stop-loss and told that if they keep a profit target of 2 percent and stop-loss at 1 percent, then it will keep the risk-reward ratio in their favour.

But remember that you will lose your entire capital of 10,000 in 20 trades even if you keep booking losses by repeatedly triggering 500-500 stop-losses. Secondly, stop-losses are not triggered when there is a sudden large drop. For example, if your stock is at 10.50 and you have placed a stop loss of 10.20, then in a major fall, it straightaway goes from 10.50 to 9.90. In such a situation, if the price of 10.20 is not reached, your stop-loss will not be triggered and you can incur a huge loss even though you have a stop loss.

So, overall, the gist is that you should work in stocks only after understanding the risk in exposure and leverage.

Avoid Over-Trading: One of the biggest mistakes that new traders make in the stock market is to make their situation worse by trading too much in a single day.

It can also be called averaging. For example, if a new trader takes a long position in a stock and the stock starts falling instead of rising, then he buys more shares at a lower rate. After that when the stock falls, then that person takes it to heart and thinks, 'Whatever happens, I cannot lose. After all, how much will it fall? At some time during the day, it will come back with an incentive.' Thinking like this, he starts buying more shares at the fallen rate. Unfortunately, if the stock doesn't rise again that day (and it doesn't rise because your over-position is being seen on the screen by the big traders), then at the end of the day you incur an enormous loss.

So, the first point is that you should not make a habit of sitting in front of the screen all day trading segments like intraday, futures option etc. If you are a full-time trader and want to trade in these segments, then you should have a specific goal in your mind as to at what price you will enter and at what price you will exit.

You should also have a target as to how much capital you have for this segment. How much capital would you invest in a position? What will you do if that trade doesn't work out in your favour? Will you have any remaining capital for the second position? My maths about this is pretty straightforward. I also give a similar opinion to my followers and readers. Divide the amount of capital you want to invest in the stock market by 33. 1/33 of the total capital is the amount you should invest in a trade.

For example, if someone tells me that they want to invest ₹ 5,00,000 lakhs in the stock market and asks about the amount they should invest in a share. So, I tell him that the amount obtained by dividing 5,00,000 by 33 is 15,151.51 and that is the amount they should invest in one share at a time.

With this, even if you have to hold 33 shares in case the market falls, you will not lose your capital. If you book a profit of 3.5 percent even after taking trade of 15,151.51, then it is a profit of about ₹ 530, which is not less. If you book a profit of 500-500 20,000 times, then your total profit will be ₹ 1 crore rupees.

❑

2
Important Rules to Know in the Stock Market

The wise investor is the realist, who sells to the optimists and buys from the pessimists.

–Benjamin Graham

In this chapter, you will be told some basic essential rules to make a profit from investment in the stock market.

Is it necessary for an investor to have a separate bank account? Generally, as an investor, you should have a savings account in any bank with a core banking solution. In any case, most banks nowadays have Core Banking Solution or CBS facility.

Now the question is whether the savings account that you already have, in which your salary or other savings are deposited, is sufficient or you will have to open a separate savings account for investment? The simple answer is that by linking any savings account with CBS (i.e. Online Banking) facility to your trading account, you can trade or invest in the stock market. But my advice to you is that instead of using the savings account that you use for everyday use, you should open another savings account especially for depositing capital for investment, and link that savings account with your trading account for this investment.

Following are the reasons to open a separate savings account for investment:

1. As I recommend my followers to read the book The Richest Man of Babylon and if you have also read my book How Abdul Became Hero from Zero in Share Bazar, then you would know as mentioned in both these books that we should save 10 percent of our income regularly and increase it continuously by investing it. If you do this with sincerity and discipline, then you are sure to become rich due to the compounding effect of your savings and their return on investment.
2. This maintains discipline in investing. It lets you know clearly the amount you have set aside for investment.
3. Whatever income from dividends will be deposited in this account or the additional amount that you will bring into this account from the trading account, you will be able to keep track of it and you will be able to add dividends etc. easily while filing the income tax return.
4. Further in this book, in the chapter on Earning from Mutual Funds, I have described the I-method to earn regular monthly income by investing in NiftyBees or Index ETFs, which is facilitated by having a separate bank account.

How Having a Trading Account with a Broker Works: You must have seen the web series based on Harshad Mehta. (If you haven't seen it, you should watch it. You will get to learn a lot from it.) In this, you must have seen how in the past, bids had to be shouted out among the crowd in the market and written to buy and sell shares. But now the whole system has gone online. Now when you open a trading account with your broker, the broker takes a 'power of attorney' from you and you can place orders to buy and sell on the broker's online trading platform or the broker's app.

With the Power of Attorney, the broker agrees with you that he will place the order in accordance with the online or phone order placed by you and will not make any changes on his own.

Do Not Ignore the Risk: When they invest in the stock market, most investors or traders are very excited about the return on their investment or trade. But they mostly don't consider the risk involved at all.

Therefore, while deciding to invest, do not just think about the extent of loss that you will incur on this investment. You must ask yourself that if there is a loss in this investment, then are you in a position to bear that loss? Or do you have a strategy that will allow you to exit the stock even after incurring a loss?

Various Factors Due to which You Can Incur Losses: Always remember that you may have to suffer losses in your stock market investments because of the following factors:

(1) Financial crisis, (2) Decline in the economy, (3) Political uncertainty, (4) Various scams, (5) Loss of option for the production in a company, (6) Any kind of government ban on the company, etc., (7) Situation like war or epidemic arising.

Always avoid over-zealousness keeping in mind that your investments may be at risk due to the reasons mentioned. So, always remember that never invest more than 1/33 of your total capital in a single share.

Take responsibility for your investments: You should get as much information as possible about the shares and the financial position of the company. You should not invest in hot tips based on the tips received from brokers, friends, relatives, SMS tips, tips received from a telegram channel or YouTube channels, hot tips based on rumours doing rounds on Facebook and WhatsApp groups because, in most cases, the investors who invest in these tips have been seen incurring losses.

Trust the investment advice of a SEBI registered research analysts; however, don't rely on them blindly. I myself am a registered and NISM certified Research Analyst. But that doesn't mean that the stock that I mention will go up. Depending on the market conditions, the stock may fall instead of going up. That's why you should always have a strategy as to what you would do if the stock falls. That's why I recommend investing by the STP method in whatever investment advice I give on my blog. In this method, the shares are bought in small pieces rather than all at once and each purchase is made when the highest level of the last 15 calendar days is triggered. That's why it is called STP or ShareGenius Trigger Point Method.

Before investing on the basis of the research reports of SEBI Registered Research Analysts, do your own research and remember – we Research Analysts are investors and human beings just like you. So, our report can also go wrong. Therefore, on the basis of the risk factors mentioned, when the market falls, do not invest too much in the best stock and invest only a small amount in the stock.

Therefore, at the time of any investment, make a strategy to deal with the possible losses/risks in advance so that if the investment goes in the opposite direction, then you can exit safely without blaming anyone. Two strategies are adopted for a safe exit from a falling investment: (1) the stop-loss strategy, and (2) the averaging strategy.

1. **Averaging Loss Strategy:** In this strategy, after the investment falls to a certain percentage, the loss from it is reconciled. With this strategy, losses can be limited. But loss is loss after all. If your stop-loss is triggered repeatedly, you will slowly end up losing a huge amount. That's why I never encourage a stop-loss strategy.
2. **Averaging Strategy:** In this strategy, by buying the falling shares in higher quantity, an attempt is made to reduce the

buying-price average of the shares so that when there is a slight rise or bounce back, one can exit the stock without any loss. If this method is also applied with ignorance, that is, by averaging quickly without following any rules, then it is very dangerous and you will not even know when your big money will get stuck as you average time and again.

Therefore, to get out of falling investments, instead of the methods suggested, use 'Darvas Box Theory', 'STP Method' or 'Smart Averaging Method' and invest in parts and gradually do regular average with these methods. These methods will be described in subsequent chapters of the book.

Do Not Fall into the Trap of Penny Stocks: Most of the investors want to earn more in the short term and such a desire misleads even good investors. Sometimes even good investors end up investing in cheap stocks of worthless small companies or companies with weak fundamentals that have been making losses for a long time.

Such shares are called penny shares. In fact, investors invest in it like buying a lottery ticket and they feel that the penny company they have invested in is going to grow a lot in the times to come. But 99 percent of penny stocks do not show such easy movement. For this, I would advise you to read a book called The Alchemist. This book has been translated into 83 languages around the world and has sold 23 million copies. You must read this book (The Alchemist). In this, you will find many informative sayings. I will give a summary of this book to explain why I linked this book with penny share trading.

The book The Alchemist tells the story of a shepherd, who is in search of treasure (just like you are looking to earn crores of rupees from penny stocks). This shepherd has a recurring dream that on crossing the inaccessible desert, he will find treasure in the pyramids. It is the same as you hear time and again that a certain stock has increased so much that if you had bought it, you would have become a millionaire.

When the shepherd reaches the pyramid in the end after crossing many hurdles and starts digging the pyramid, he is caught by a group of desert fighters or bandits. They start beating him and asking him about why he was digging the pyramid. The boy (shepherd) tells them that he was digging pyramids for treasure. So, the robbers stop there and make him continue digging pyramids while they keep beating him. But even after digging extensively, they can't find the treasure (like you see your penny stocks going down, but you don't find the treasure).

In the end, the chief of the dacoits asks him how he knew that there was a treasure there. So, the boy tells him that he had a recurring dream that there was a treasure here. The chief of the dacoits laughs. Together they again beat him badly and leave him to die. Then the chief of the dacoits brings the half-dead man back to his senses and says, 'Stupid boy, just as you had a dream, I also had a dream that a shepherd tends his sheep across this desert. There is a treasure under the poplar tree under which he sits. But I was not a fool like you to go there taking such a risk.'

In fact, the boy tended to the sheep sitting under a poplar tree and the chief of the robbers had told him the correct address of the treasure. After hearing that, he went back and took out the treasure.

Just as that shepherd, after working so hard and being half-dead came to know that the treasure was in the same place where he used to sit every day, in the same way, instead of investing in penny shares, I will give you the easy address of the treasure to earn crores of rupees. I found this address in my attempt of 17 years to find treasure in the stock market like that shepherd, which I am going to tell you about in a moment.

Basically, stop trying to earn crores in a single share like a lottery and keep your focus only on booking a profit of ₹ 500 in any trade. If you make 20,000 trades in which you have booked a profit of ₹ 500, then your total profit will be ₹ 1 crore. For those who do not believe, they can confirm by multiplying 20,000 by 500 in the calculator. Now also keep in mind that this is not 20,000 days, i.e. I have not said that by earning ₹ 500 rupees daily, you will earn 1 crore in 20,000 days. I sometimes book ₹ 500 rupees in trades and earn ₹ 4500 in a single day. But I believe that by booking ₹ 500 in 20,000 trades, the treasury of 1 crore will be full like the shepherd. So, the summary is that leaving the lure of earning crores from a single penny share, keep booking small profits and keep reinvesting the original capital.

How do we start trading in a stock market? This big fundamental question is asked by newbies. To get started in the stock market, you must first understand that you should not compare it with gambling, betting, and lotteries. You should not consider it as a quick money-making tool. You have to build a long relationship in the stock market. Therefore, pledge from the beginning that you will continue to learn in the stock market with eagerness and readiness by maintaining your interest and you will stay away from greed and fear.

❑

3

The Process for Opening a Demat Account

A Demat account is basically an electronic account, where all your shares are deposited in a dematerialized format. There was a time, when people used to buy shares from the stock market and keep them in the respective files. With the advent of digitalization, online trading has changed the way traders and investors hold/deposit shares. In short, it becomes necessary to have a Demat account for doing business. For this, you can start looking for the right broker, who provides specialized services to you.

In general, all stocks are listed on the stock exchange (NSE, Nifty or BSE Sensex). Learn how to open an NSE account to start investing in the stock market. When you buy shares on the stock exchange, you pay your monetary amount against the shares and then your shares get credited in the Demat account. Once you sell these shares, the number of shares belonging to the same Demat account is deducted and you get the amount received from the sale.

Apart from stocks, you can deposit other investment products, such as ETFs (Exchange Traded Funds), mutual funds, government securities, bonds, etc.

Various stockbrokers charge Demat account charges as well as Demat account maintenance charges. You have to pay the cost of opening the account once. Annual Maintenance Charges or AMC is a recurring cost, which has to be paid every year.

These Demat accounts are basically provided through two regulated depositories CDSL or NSDL. Various stockbrokers or depository participants are members of one or both the above-mentioned depositories.

A Demat account is like your bank account. Just like you deposit your money in a savings or existing account with a bank in a non-physical or electronic form, the shares you buy from the stock market get credited to your Demat account in an electronic form.

Demat Account: The Basics

- A Demat account will be linked to your PAN card.
- You can open as many Demat accounts as you want with different stockbrokers. But it has advantages and disadvantages depending on your trading style.
- A unique ID number will be linked to your Demat account, which basically differentiates you from other investors in the stock market.
- Not every stockbroker has the provision to open a Demat account directly. At the backend, such shareholders have partnerships with other depository participants who actually open your Demat account.
- Shares can be transferred from one Demat account to another.
- You do not have to open your Demat account with minimum shares or maintain minimum shares balance in your account.

Purposes of Demat Account

- All the shares in these accounts are held in electronic or dematerialized form.
- Investors can hold not only shares, but also mutual funds, ETFs, government bonds and securities.
- The shares held in the account are protected and kept away from risks such as theft, loss or damage.
- It provides an easy online mechanism to view, transfer, sell or buy various investment products through a single account.

How to Open a Demat Account

- If you open a Demat account offline, you will be given an account opening form by your stockbroker. You will need to enter some basic details in the form, such as name, address, contact information, required signature, etc. Nowadays, one can open an online Demat account in just 15 minutes and you will be informed about the process later.
- The staff of the stockbroker chosen by you will provide you with the Demat account agreement, details of payment and charges to be paid and documents for the power of attorney. You are advised to read, verify and sign all the documents before handing them over to the broker.
- You have to pay an account opening fee, which is a one-time fee. In addition, there will be annual maintenance charges levied on your account. Check these details before going ahead with the opening of the account.
- Once the documents are validated by the stockbroker, they will be verified by another such person through mail or through an online call.

- After all the above documents and procedures are taken care of, you will be assigned a Demat account number by the stockbroker, which will act as the identity for your account.
- Your client ID will also be specified for the stockbroker's records.
- You will also be provided with the login credentials of various trading platforms like the mobile trading app, terminal software, etc. which you will use for trading in the stock market.

To make a start in the stock market, you will need three things

1. Aadhar Card
2. PAN Card
3. Cheque Book or Bank Statement

1. **Aadhar Card:** At present the Aadhar Card has become a basic requirement and most people already have an Aadhar card. If you do not have one, then you can go to the nearest e-Mitra and get the Aadhar card made.
2. **PAN Card:** The PAN card is the most important step in your journey towards the stock market. You can get a PAN card made online by visiting the website of NSDL yourself. To make a PAN card, you may need your Aadhar card, address proof, proof of date of birth and two photographs. Nowadays, photographs are also taken by NSDL automatically from the data of the Aadhar card. Its fee is around ₹ 110 (when this book was written in 2022) which you have to pay online.
3. **Cheque Book or Bank Statement:** When you apply for a Demat account, your broker will ask you for a cancelled cheque or a scanned copy of the bank statement.

Selecting a Stockbrokers: Now you have to select a stockbroker. There are two types of stockbrokers: 1. Full-Service Sharebroker, 2. Discount Sharebroker.

Full-Service Stockbrokers are usually banks or large brokerage firms with offices in almost all major cities. Discount stockbrokers are online brokers who have their headquarters in only one city and all their other services are online. They either do not have branches or have very few branches. Now, opening a Demat account with a full-service broker costs you more brokerage and charges, whereas discount stockbrokers get your trade done at less brokerage and charges. I personally would not recommend any broker's name to you. But you can do a comparative study on the basis of the following points while choosing a stockbroker:

1. What are their brokerage charges?
2. What is the quality of the platform/app available for business?
3. How effective is the customer care/customer service facility? You can call customer care to get an idea of how the customer service operates or functions.
4. Geographical reach i.e., whether the broker has any nearest office or not.
5. Market research and suggestions, i.e., how is the broker's research recommendation.
6. Trading Margin, i.e., how much margin the broker provides for delivery base trading and at what rate he charges interest on the margin. Margin here means that some brokers also lend you an amount to buy shares at low interest, which is called margin. You can take delivery of the shares by repaying this loan amount anytime within 365 days. For more information, you can also watch my video on MTF trading by searching 'MTF' 'Trading Mahesh Kaushik' on YouTube.

7. Business Segment, i.e., whether the broker provides services in all the segments or not. For example, there is a segment in the market called SLB, also known as Security Lending and Borrowing. In this, you can earn monthly rent by lending the shares held in your Demat account. But many brokers do not provide services in the SLB segment or charge exorbitant rents.
8. Conduct/History of the stockbroker: For how many years your stockbroker has been working and how reliable he is – you can easily research it on the internet and choose an experienced and reliable broker.

Thus, you should choose the broker on the basis of these points, and also ensure whether you will earn money by trading continuously or if you want to make money by becoming a long-term investor. After that, your next step should be to open a Demat account.

Opening an Online Demat Account: After selecting a broker, you can sign-up online on the broker's website. In case of any sign-up issues, you can contact the broker's customer care and on receiving your contact number, the broker's representative will call you and assist you in opening the Demat account. Nowadays, the process of opening a Demat account has become online. After entering your PAN number and Aadhaar number, the broker's firm, with the help of the DigiLocker, completes the process of E-KYC by sending an OTP on the mobile linked with your Aadhar and your Demat account gets activated in one to two days.

What is POA and Why it is Necessary: When you open an online Demat account, your broker will request you to sign a POA i.e., Power of Attorney and physically mail it to the broker's office. Now even if you do not send that power of attorney, your Demat account will be activated. However, you will have to enter the PIN number received from NSDL or CDSL every time you sell the shares. Also, if you want the facility of margin trading i.e.

trading by borrowing money from the broker, you still need to sign and send this POA. Further in this book, you will also be told about the facility of taking margin at zero interest.

Basic Knowledge of the Stock Market: Apart from opening a Demat account, there is another important step – you need to get the basic knowledge of the stock market. You can study that by visiting some free websites like Investopedia, Varsity that provide basic knowledge of the stock market. By the way, in this book, you will get more knowledge on this subject. Apart from this, you can also read my other books published by Prabhat Prakashan.

Watch the Market: Prepare a list of 20 to 30 major stocks to invest in. For this, I would advise you to choose the companies with the highest market cap. You can select the top 20 companies with the highest market cap by searching Top Companies by Market Cap on Google and visiting Money Control's website. Then study their daily movement and historical movement. Tracking 20 stocks in a row will help you understand the nuances of the market and on what and why the market movements depend.

Personal Strategy: Now choose a personal strategy for your investment. Various strategies will be suggested to you in the subsequent chapters of the book. You can choose the strategy for yourself from among them.

❑

4
Learn to Read Financial Statements

Before you learn to read financial statements, make sure you save at least 10 percent of your salary and invest it regularly in the stock market. Most people deposit their savings in the form of RD or FD in the bank so that they do not have to borrow money from anyone during hard times. But the 5 to 7 percent interest rate on bank FD or RD is not enough to beat the inflation rate, due to which the value of your savings decreases continuously in the future. So, you have to invest in real estate, gold, or the stock market to get higher returns on your savings.

You will be happy to know that with the help of your Demat account, you can invest your money in the stock market, real estate, and also gold with the help of ETFs and mutual funds, which we will learn in detail later. To get started in the stock market, we need very little money. If you have stock market skills, then you can buy a part of someone's business in the form of some shares.

Warren Buffett, who is the world's richest investor, had said that those who do not know how to read financial statements, should not invest in stocks. This statement of Warren Buffett is absolutely correct. Today, in this chapter, I am going to teach you a very simple way to read financial statements. So, let's get started. Suppose Nitin wants to start a company, which will sell buffalo ghee. Nitin has the whole concept in mind – he will raise buffaloes, make ghee from their milk and sell it under the brand name 'Mahadev Desi Ghee' with good packaging and advertising. He has also named his company as 'Mahadev Desi Ghee'.

Now Nitin needs ₹ 10 lakhs to start this business. Nitin is a sensible businessman. He thinks why should I invest all of my own money in this business? He wants to invest only ₹ 5 lakh rupees. So, for this, he forms a limited company, which he names 'Mahadev Desi Ghee Limited'. He keeps the total net worth of the company at ₹ 10 lakhs, out of which he borrows ₹ 3 lakhs from his friend Suresh Patel. In return for this finance, he gives a certificate to Suresh Patel that Nitin will return him ₹ 3 lakhs with interest after a certain period (this certificate will be called a bond). If Nitin had borrowed ₹ 3 lakhs from a bank, it would have been called a loan. But Nitin borrows from his friend without taking a loan from the bank. In return, he issues a bond to pay him back ₹ 3 lakhs with interest.

Now for the remaining ₹ 7 lakhs, Nitin makes 70,000 shares of his company at a face value of ₹ 10 each and becomes the owner of 50,000 shares by investing his ₹ 5 lakh. This is a promoter's holding of 50,000 shares as Nitin is the promoter of his company. Now he gives the remaining 2 lakhs shares (20,000 shares of the face value of ₹ 10) to another friend Raghuveer in exchange for ₹ 2 lakhs. So, now let us make the balance sheet of Nitin's company. There are two main aspects in the balance sheet of a company:

1. Assets
2. Liabilities

Assets include cash, company's property and machinery, etc. Liabilities include things that the company has to pay to someone, such as bank loans, loans taken against bonds or money collected from equity, which have to be given back to the shareholders. On the balance sheet of a company, the assets are on the left side and liabilities are on the right side. Now if we look at Nitin's balance sheet, then his assets will be on the left side, where there is a stock of 10 lakh buffaloes and 100 litres of desi ghee, whose market value is 50,000 at the rate of ₹ 500 per kg and his machinery or tools (which are buffaloes here) worth ₹ 10 lakhs and 50,000 worth of desi ghee.

Liabilities are on the right side of his balance sheet, which has shares of ₹ 7 lakhs and bonds of ₹ 3 lakhs. Remember here that Nitin himself also has a liability of ₹ 5 lakh shares under liabilities. Now you will think that when the company belongs to Nitin, then how did his 5 lakh shares become the liability of the company? In fact, Nitin and the company are legally separate entities. Therefore, the company has a liability to pay ₹ 5 lakhs to Nitin as well. Today, you must have understood how rich people take advantage of this subtlety in law. This means that he did not have to spend anything and still his mission is fulfilled. That is, Nitin has actually become the owner of a company worth ₹ 10 lakhs by investing zero rupees.

Now you will ask how it is zero rupees as Nitin has invested ₹ 5 lakhs in the company? Actually, the shares are the liability of the company, i.e., the company has to pay ₹ 5 lakhs to Nitin. Now suppose that unfortunately, Nitin's company goes bankrupt. Due to the severe flood, half of Nitin's buffaloes die and the ghee stock also gets spoiled and has to be thrown away or discarded. In these adverse circumstances, on auctioning the remaining buffaloes, Nitin gets only ₹ 3 lakhs. So, who will get this ₹ 3 lakhs? This ₹ 3 lakhs will go to Nitin's friend Suresh Patel, who bought the bonds by paying ₹ 3 lakhs. This is so because when any company goes bankrupt, the bond owner gets the money first after the company's assets are sold. After that, come the shareholders. Therefore, bonds are safer than shares.

Here, when the company was sold, all the money went to the bondholders and nothing was left for the shareholders. Hence the shareholder's capital has become zero. You should also pay close attention to the liquidity of the company's assets while reading a company's balance sheet. Suppose there are two companies, A and B. The 'A' company has assets of ₹ 10 lakhs. The assets of the company 'B' are ₹ 8 lakhs.

Now if the shares of both the companies are trading at the same price and you are asked which company is good for investment, then you should not take a decision directly in favour of A by looking at its assets. Suppose out of ₹ 10 lakhs of A's assets, there is old machinery worth ₹ 8 lakhs and cash and gold worth ₹ 2 lakhs, while in B's assets, there is new machinery worth ₹ 4 lakhs and cash and gold worth ₹ 4 lakhs, then you have to focus on liquidity. The cash and gold worth ₹ 4 lakhs that Company B has is more liquid and if companies go bankrupt, then B company's new machinery will get more money than A and its gold and cash of ₹ 4 lakhs will also be easily liquidated. Therefore, always choose a company for investment, which has high liquidity of assets.

Warren Buffett's Principle of Margin of Safety: Warren Buffett says that you should always buy a company at a cheaper rate than its real value and not risk your principal because then the magic of the power of compounding will not work for you if you lose the principal. That is, if you invest money in a bad company, where your money is reduced to less than half, then by the time you recover the principal, the investors investing in good companies will have doubled their money.

According to old-time big investors like Buffett, Graham etc., buying a company for less than its book value is a value buy. But nowadays the world is dominated by lies, cunning and fraud. Therefore, to show the value in their balance sheets, companies show such assets in the asset column, which have very little real value. For example, a company is showing intangible assets of ₹ 18 lakhs on its balance sheet.

If you go to the bottom of the income of this intangible asset, you learn that the company has spent ₹ 18 lakhs on its advertisements and those advertisements will bring customers for them. Hence ₹ 18 lakhs advertisements are its intangible asset. Now think if this company goes bankrupt, will we be able to raise ₹ 18 lakhs by selling 18 lakh advertisements? Advertisement is not a real asset. It cannot be sold in a bankruptcy case. So, beware of false book value.

To avoid this, I do not use the concept of trading at less than book value in the value buy share that I mention on my blog.

I use the concept of trading below the stock on net sell instead. For example, if the total number of shares of a company 'A' is ₹ 1 lakhs and its total sale is ₹ 10 lakhs, then the sale of a share would come to ₹ 10. But the number of shares of a company 'B' is 2 lakhs and its sale is ₹ 12 lakhs, then the sale of a share would come to only ₹ 6. So, I will consider company A as a value buy in compared to B even though the sale of company 'A' is less because it gets more share of sales per share.

For example, there are 500 shops in a town. Let's say each shop is a company. Then if we arrange these 500 shops on the basis of their annual sales, then there are the top 50 shops, which have the highest sales out of the total 500 shops, more likely to distance themselves from their business or will the last 50 shops with the lowest sales close down?

You must have understood that the last 50 shops, which have the lowest sales, can close their business. Exactly the same thing applies to the stock market as well. There are about 3,500 listed companies here. But only about 1,000 of them are such companies, whose sale per share is more than their market price. That's why I recommend buying shares in the form of value buy only from companies whose market price is less than their sales per share.

Annual Sales Per Share: By dividing the number of shares of a company by the annual sales of that company, we get annual sales per share.

Assume that the annual sale of company 'A' is ₹ 336.25 crores and the total shares of the company are ₹ 12.24 crores. So, its annual price per share is ₹ 336.28 crores (Total Sales) / ₹ 12.24 crores (Total Share) = 27.47.

Now if this share is available at less than this price, that is, less than ₹ 27, then it is getting cheaper, otherwise, it is getting expensive. This is my simple maths. Annual sale per share is my first favourite checkpoint from which I first estimate the valuation of a stock.

Now, this does not mean at all that the share of Company 'A' will not trade above ₹ 27. You can see it trading at ₹ 270 and even at 2,700 because the stock market prices are not based on the fundamentals of the company. They are based on demand and supply. If Company 'A' has more buyers and fewer sellers and buyers want to pay more, then the market price can go over ₹ 27, and you can get an idea from the annual sales per share that you are buying at a higher price. Someday, if the sales of the company do not rise and the buyers become fewer and the sellers increase, then the stock may fall below ₹ 27. So, my first advice is to replace the old concept of book value with the new concept of annual sales per share to see if the share is a value buy or not.

If you want to know more about Financial Statements, you can read the book The Interpretation of Financial Statements by Benjamin Graham.

❑

5
Meaning of Words Prevalent in the Stock Market

"Consider the ups and downs of the market your friend. Take advantage of the stupidity of others, don't be a part of it."

–Warren Buffett

The shares of a company basically divide the ownership of the company. This means that a company's shares represent a share in its assets and earnings. When a company is incorporated, some initial investors may be made shareholders. Later on, as the company grows and more money is needed for expansion, the company may issue more shares to other investors. Now, I will try to explain to you the meaning of some of the popular words about shares in the stock market. There are two types of shares on the basis of dividends:

1. **Common Stock:** Usually the shares you buy and sell are the common stock of the company. The common stockholders receive dividends declared by the company periodically and the common shareholders also vote to elect the board of investors.

2. **Preferred Stock:** In preferred stock or preferential shares, a fixed amount of dividend is paid every year to the shareholders. There are also different types of preferred

stock. It is enough for you as a common investor to know that you cannot buy and sell preferred stocks directly from the stock market. Preferred stocks are issued directly by companies to large investors with the promise of higher dividends or a fixed annual dividend. However, shareholders of preferred stock may or may not have voting rights to elect a board of investors like common stockholders.

Types of Shares on the Basis of Market Capitalization: First we should understand the market capitalization or market cap. Suppose the market value of a share is ₹ 300 and the company has a total of 1,00,000 shares. So, multiplying the market value of that company (300) by the number of shares (1,00,000) of that company gives ₹ 3 crores, which is the market cap or market capitalization of that company. In a nutshell, the market cap of a share multiplied by the number of its total shares, or the market value of the total number of shares of the company, is called its market capitalization. There are three types of shares on the basis of market cap:

1. Large Cap Stocks
2. Mid Cap Stocks
3. Small Cap Stocks

1. **Large Cap Stocks:** The shares of companies whose market capital is more than ₹ 20,000 crores are called Large Cap Stocks. The market cap of Reliance's stock in India (in 2022) is the highest. Apart from this, there are companies like TCS, Infosys, HDFC Bank, Hindustan Unilever, ITC, L&T, HDFC, Kotak Mahindra Bank, ICICI Bank etc., whose market cap is several lakh crores.

   In fact, having a higher market cap means that most of the stock market money is invested in these large caps. From that, you can understand that these are established and big companies in their area. Owing to their large number of shares, their prices do not fluctuate much. Therefore, these shares are considered safe for investment. If you are a new investor, then you should invest only in large cap companies (whose market cap is more than ₹ 20,000 crores).

2. **Mid Cap Stocks:** The companies whose market capital is between ₹ 5,000 crores to 20,000 crores are called mid cap companies. Investing in these companies is riskier as compared to large caps as their prices rise quickly due to a smaller number of shares. But at the time of decline, they also fall sharply and sometimes they are less than half of their high price. The risk involved in them is high. Nevertheless, investors invest in them with the expectation that in the future these companies will become large cap companies, and fortunately, if this happens, then the price of their stock also increases manifold.

3. **Small Cap Stocks:** All stocks with a market cap of less than ₹ 5,000 crores are called small cap stocks. These are usually start-ups or companies that are in the early stages of development. Due to their small number of shares, their prices are easily manipulated by increasing demand artificially at times, allowing small investors to easily get trapped in them and lose most of their money. If you are a new investor, then you should stay away from small caps or avoid investing in them without understanding the fundamentals of the company.

Stocks on the Basis of Sharing of Profits Between the Shareholders by the Companies

There are 2 types of shares on the basis of sharing of profits among the shareholders:

1. Income Stocks
2. Growth Stocks

1. **Income Stock:** Such companies, which have been distributing dividends from time to time to their investors for many years continuously come under Income Stock. These are also called 'high dividend chilled companies' or 'high dividend paying stocks'. Since these companies distribute profits from time to time in the form of dividends, their value does not increase much. For example, IOC is an income stock, which pays handsome dividends to the shareholders periodically. It is a stable large-cap company. But remember – this does not mean that you blindly buy IOC for regular income. Always remember – everything is uncertain in the stock market. Therefore, IOC may not pay regular dividends in the future.

   For example, between 2010 and 2015, state-run banks (PNB) etc., paid fairly regular dividends to their investors. But later their shares fell and because of the unexpected increase in NPAs of banks, etc., their market prices also fell to less than one-fourth. Instead of profit, they gave rise to losses. After 2016, dividend distribution stopped in public sector banks that had been giving dividends continuously.

   Now it can also start again when they become profitable in the future. What I mean is that if a stock is an income stock today, it may not remain so tomorrow. That's why you have to invest smartly in the stock market. Don't worry. As you continue to read my book (and other books) and learn by watching videos on my YouTube channel, you will learn to make regular profits.

2. **Growth Stocks:** These are stocks that despite getting dividends, either do not distribute dividends or pay marginal dividends as they spend their income on the expansion of the company (opening new branches of the company, investment in new businesses), etc. This may not give you a

direct dividend. But as the company continues to grow, you get the benefit of its increasing market price.

For example, Reliance is one such stock, which distributes fewer dividends. But in the last few years, the market value of Reliance has increased from ₹ 51.95 on November 8, 2002 to ₹ 2,407.95 in the year 2022.

Types of Stocks Based on Intrinsic Value: Intrinsic value means the intrinsic value of the company, i.e., the benefit that we can get from the company in the future is intrinsic value. There is no set formula for its calculation. This concept has been popularized by renowned investor Warren Buffett. But since the common investors cannot calculate it and it is not possible to predict the future cash flow accurately. I consider it more appropriate to make investment decisions by comparing the market value of the company with the net sales per share instead of investing on the basis of intrinsic value. Nevertheless, for your information, there are two types of shares on the basis of intrinsic value:

1. **Overvalued Stocks:** Those that are trading at a market value higher than the intrinsic value.
2. **Undervalued Stocks:** Those that are trading at a market value below the intrinsic value.

Meaning of Some Common Terms Prevalent in the Stock Market

1. **Cyclic Stocks:** The price of shares of some companies increases when the economy is doing well and decreases when the economy is weak. Such stocks are called cyclic stocks. For example, stocks of automobile companies.
2. **Defensive Stock:** The stocks which do not fall much even when the market falls are called defensive stocks. For example, food companies (Hindustan Lever, ITC, Dabur), pharma companies, insurance companies etc.

3. **Blue-Chip Stocks:** Established companies with stable earnings that give consistent dividends or make good growth are called blue-chip companies. Generally, you can call the stocks included in Nifty 50 or Sensex blue-chip shares.

4. **High Beta Stocks:** Stocks that rise more when the market rises and slips more when the market is down are called high beta stocks. That is, the volatility of high beta stocks is higher than the market. Therefore, investing in them is considered unsafe. Stocks with low beta are considered safe for investment as they are less volatile.

Summary: Do not worry if you are unable to understand the various above-mentioned terms after reading them. The purpose of the said terms is only to let you know that you should always use diversification in the stock market so that you can keep your invested amount safe.

You must have heard a famous saying – 'Don't put all your eggs in one basket'. This proverb unintentionally describes the protection from risk with diversification.

So, always remember my formula that you should not invest more than 1/33 of your total investible capital in 1 share. Now if your total capital is 3.30 lakhs, then it is natural that you should not invest more than ₹ 10,000 in a share. So, buy shares worth ₹ 10 thousand each of 33 companies and keep rotating the capital by earning small profits from them. With this, you can easily keep earning continuously.

❑

6
How Do Stock Prices Change?

"When investors do not understand what they are doing, then only wide diversification is needed."

–Warren Buffett

When a company goes public, it issues stocks or shares to the general public to raise funds from the market. These shares are bought and sold by individuals, corporations, banks etc. on stock exchanges like NSE, BSE, etc. But the common investor is always surprised to know that some stocks of different companies rise and some fall at the same time. Not only this, the value of the stock either increases or decreases in an instant. In this chapter, let us understand how stock prices change. First of all, you should understand that the market value of a stock is made up of two factors:

(1) Face Value

(2) Premium

For example, the market price of Reliance's share is 2,461.85 and the face value of Reliance's shares is ₹ 10. So, here 2,451.85 is at a premium. This means that for buying a par stake of ₹ 10 in Reliance, you are buying this share for 10 + 2,451.85 = 2,461.85 by paying a premium of 2,451.85. Most common investors think that if they are buying a share worth 2,461.85, then they are investing 2,461.85 in it. But this is wrong. In fact, on buying 1 share of Reliance, your stake in Reliance will be equal to the face value, i.e., ₹ 10 only. The remaining premium of 2,451.85 is being paid by you to the person who sold the shares to you.

Theory of Demand and Supply: If the demand for a share increases for any reason, the price of the share will increase and if the demand for the stock falls, the price of the share will fall. When demand increases, the share price rises because there are more buyers and they are prepared to buy shares by paying a higher premium because no one wants to sell shares at a lower premium due to less supply.

Suppose someone wants to buy 100 shares of Reliance at 2,461.85. On the other hand, someone wants to sell 100 shares at 2,461.85. So, the exchange executes the deal if the price of both matches. This 2,461.85 now becomes the last trading price (LTP) of the stock. Now the demand is high, but no one wants to sell their shares at less than 2,500. So, they place a sell order at 2,500. Now if a buyer places a buy order at 2,500, then the order will get executed due to the match and now the share price will increase to 2,500. So, in this way, the price of shares increases. But the face value is fixed at ₹ 10, only the premium has increased from 2,451.85 to 2,490. These transactions happen very fast. In almost every example mentioned above, multiple buyers and sellers place bids and offers in different quantities at different prices. When you go to the website of the exchange, you will see two types of prices there:

1. Bid Price
2. ASK Price

The Bid Price is the price at which a buyer wants to buy the stock and the ASK price is the price at which a seller wants to sell the stock. If a person places an order to sell a large number of shares, it is natural that he will clear orders for many bid prices.

Therefore, placing an order to sell a higher quantity of shares will result in a fall in the price of the share. Similarly, when the buy order is for more shares (if there is an order to buy the shares at the market price i.e., at any price), they will buy the shares of several proposers and absorb their offer prices. This will increase the price of the shares.

Hence the prices can rise and fall very rapidly depending on the requirement of the buyers and sellers. Now let us understand all the major factors that largely affect the value of a stock.

1. **News About the Profit and Income of the Company:** When there is news of earnings, profit, loss, or potential earnings of a company, the price of the shares appears to increase or decrease depending on whether that news is positive or negative. For example, when the company receives a new, big contract and when this news comes out, many investors buy shares with the expectation of increasing the potential earnings from this contract in the future, thereby increasing the price of the shares immediately. But I personally do not believe in buying shares on the basis of such news and would also advise you not to decide to buy/sell shares on the basis of such news. Since this is the hi-tech era and in most cases the stock prices increase/decrease even before the news comes out, it has a momentary effect after the news is announced and after that, the price goes back to the original state.

2. **Dividend, Bonus, Right Issue, etc.:** Sometimes some new investors start buying as they get excited by the companies announcing dividends, bonuses and right issues, due to which their price starts increasing in the market. But overall, my advice to you again is that do not invest just by listening to the news of dividends, bonuses and right issues because, after the expiry of their record date, the shares start losing steam that they had gathered due to the news and the prices of the shares start falling.

3. **Effect of Different Kinds of News:** Some other positive/ negative news about the above two points may also affect the price of shares temporarily, such as:

1. Business-related information, such as launching new products,
2. Errors or scams found by the auditors,
3. Estimated acquisition or merger,
4. Resignation of Directors,
5. News of layoffs, strikes and lockouts in the company,
6. Changes in ratings given to companies by brokerage houses, CRISIL and other rating agencies,
7. Macroeconomic conditions, such as the rate of inflation and the performance of the industrial index.

Thus, always remember that the original face value of the stock remains constant. This face value is the share capital invested by you in the company. The premium only fluctuates when the share price moves or fluctuates, depending on a number of news-based factors apart from demand and supply. Therefore, the movement of premiums is not a fixed rule, it depends on the correct market perception.

Basically, the premium depends on the psychology of the participants participating in the stock market. Sometimes the fundamentals of the stock are not acceptable, but the notion about shares in the market keeps the share prices artificially high. For example, in 1995, the dotcom bubble started, in which the market value of Internet-based companies increased manifold. Eventually, the dotcom bubble that had started in 1995 burst in 2001 and the prices of these companies crashed, causing enormsous losses to their investors. So, the gist is that it would be beneficial not to invest on the basis of news and market sentiment.

❑

7
Online Share Trading and its Importance

"Buy only what you can happily hold for the next ten years."

–Warren Buffett

The facility to buy and sell shares through a virtual trading platform is known as online trading. Nowadays the facility of online trading is provided by most stockbrokers. You can buy and sell not only shares but also other financial securities like Equity, Mutual Funds, IPO, Commodity, Currency, Gold, and ETFs from the online share trading platform.

Online Share Trading: When you open a Demat account, you are provided with the online share trading account ID password, etc. After that, you can trade online by visiting your broker's website or mobile app. After logging on to your broker's website or app, you will get access to the layout of the portal. The basic layout of the trading portal is almost the same. Following are the meanings of the keywords used in the layout of the trading portal:

1. **Scrip Code:** Scrip Code means – NSE or BSE Code of the share.
2. **Bid Price:** Bid Price means the price at which a buyer wants to buy a share.

3. **ASK Price:** The ASK price is the price at which a seller wants to sell his shares.

4. **GTT Order:** GTT Order stands for Good Till Trigger Order. In this, you provide a trigger price that if the stock ever hits this trigger price, then your order will be triggered. For example, the share of Company X is trading at ₹ 100. If you think that it will accelerate over 110, then you can keep the GTT at 110. As soon as the stock moves above 110, your order will be placed automatically. Similarly, if you want to buy shares during the fall and you feel that you want to buy shares for 90 instead of 100, then you can apply GTT of 90. Your order will be triggered whenever the stock drops to 90. Currently, only Zerodha and Angel One offer GTT ordering facility. Maybe other brokers will also provide this facility in the future. (GTT order is valid for one year.)

   SBI Securities has the facility of Good Till Date Order, which is similar to the GTT order, where the order that you have placed is valid for one month. If you want to provide a trigger point, the stop loss trigger price has to be entered in the good till date order.

5. **Stop Loss Trigger Price Order:** This is called the SLTP order. It works like GTT order. ICICI Direct and some other brokers provide SLTP orders. Suppose, the last trade price of a stock is ₹ 94 and you want to buy it for more than ₹ 100. My new readers would ask why we would buy the stock which is 94 for more than 100. Basically, there are technical levels of shares. It is only when the stock goes above that level that the stock becomes bullish, otherwise the falling stock keeps falling further. That's why smart investors buy shares over and above such technical levels.

   On my YouTube channel, I instructs my followers to use these highest values as trigger points by teaching them methods like Darvas box theory (the highest price of the last trading week), STP method (the highest price of the last 15 days), Turtle trading (the highest price of 55 days), Share genius trading (the highest price of the last 20 days) etc.

So, overall, the stock is trading at 94 and your trigger point is ₹ 100, i.e., you think that there will be a bullish move above ₹ 100. So, if you keep ₹ 100 SLTP, then your order will be triggered only if it goes above ₹ 100. SLTP order has to be placed daily, whereas GTT order is valid for 1 year. SBI Securities Good Till Date Order is valid for one month. Overall, watching this video on the YouTube channel of the broker whose online trading platform you are using will help you to learn how to use the portal.

6. **Benefits of Online Trading:** Before the advent of online trading platforms in the stock market, people used to call their broker or relationship manager and get their orders written. It used to take time. During all this, the stock price went up and down, errors while listening could also lead to mistakes, and the relationship manager and broker used to mislead people by giving their own advice. But now with the advent of online trading platforms, time is saved, there is no chance of error and there is no interference by the relationship manager in your decision.

7. **Practice on Online Stock Simulator:** Many companies like Money Control, Dalal Street General, Investopedia etc. provide stock simulators. In Stock Simulator, you can buy and sell stocks like in a game by investing virtual money instead of real money. Hence it is always advised to practice on stock simulators before you start trading online with real money. Not only does it give you an online trading experience, but it also lets you learn how to work on a trading portal. Also, due to virtual cash, you can trade on the simulator without the fear of losses.

❑

8
How to Deal with Losses in the Stock Market?

"Always invest for the long term and don't put all your eggs in one basket."

–Warren Buffett

No one invests in the stock market to lose money. But experiencing a loss is part of the business. Trust me, all those who have mastered the art of the stock market do not try to avoid losses. Rather they know the art of managing their losses. Therefore, before investing in the stock market, it is necessary to learn how to deal with losses. First of all, knowing about the types of losses in the stock market will help you to learn the art of dealing with them further.

Types of Losses in Stock Trading

There are 4 types of losses in the share market

1. **Notional Loss:** You bought a share for ₹ 100 and unfortunately its market value fell to ₹ 70. Now let me ask you how much money did you lose? Perhaps your answer would be that you lost ₹ 30. But this answer is wrong because till you do not sell your shares, then this loss is only on paper and it is not an actual loss. In terms of the share market, this is called 'Notional Loss'.

I will explain in more detail. Suppose you buy a plot of land worth ₹ 15 lakhs. Now I offer to buy that plot from you for ₹ 12 lakhs. Since you have bought the plot of land for ₹ 15 lakhs and you do not sell it to me for ₹ 12 lakhs at a loss of ₹ 3 lakhs, did you lose ₹ 3 lakhs just with my offer? Let's think even further. Your neighbouring plot owner sells me the plot for ₹ 12 lakhs. (In the language of the stock market, ₹ 12 lakh was the last trading price.) So, did you still incur a loss of ₹ 3 lakhs? No, unless you sell your plot to me for ₹ 12 lakhs, the loss of ₹ 3 lakhs based on the offer price or LTP will only be the notional loss. This is the most dangerous aspect for small investors in the stock market.

Now you will ask how is that? Come, let's understand this. You will often buy a share, and it will fall and show some notional loss. You will wisely hold it thinking that it is an imaginary loss and nothing will happen and it will be so. The market will go up, you will book a profit by selling. After doing this frequently in the stock market, you will stop being afraid of notional loss. Sometimes it will so happen that your stock will gradually fall by 50-60 percent and you will not even know. Still, people making a profit would keep selling shares, and people with notional losses will keep holding. Due to this, if the shares with notional loss are of substandard companies, then they will gradually fall to 60-70 percent. Then you will realize that 70 percent of your capital has been wiped out and the shares that are left are so bad that there is no hope of their rising.

Therefore, in the stock market, the concept of stop-loss is spoken about. You should bear in mind that you will not incur more than 10 percent loss in one share and will save 90 percent capital by booking the loss. You will see most investors and traders in the market advocating stop-loss. But I am strongly against stop-loss. The following are the reasons for this:

1. Stop loss is for intraday and futures options traders and not for long-term investors or investors doing investment trading (a variant of short-term trading) in good stocks.
2. If you buy shares of top blue-chip companies, then there is no justification for booking loss by keeping stop-loss in it. Instead of selling at a loss during the fall in the shares of blue-chip companies, you can easily recover the loss with my smart averaging method.
3. I don't think anyone would want to work further in the stock market by losing 50 percent of their capital. So, the overall point is that it is foolish to convert this notional loss into an actual loss, where you will have regrets when the stock recovers later. To manage this, I have powerful methods like Smart Averaging Method, and the 200 DMA Averaging Method, which will be described later. For now, let's understand other types of losses:

2. **Capital Loss or Actual Loss:** When you sell a share at a price less than its purchase price, you incur a capital loss or actual loss. As I have mentioned above, if you keep the stock when the price is falling, it keeps adding to your losses. I do not encourage my followers to book actual losses. But it is not much harmful to book the actual loss due to two reasons-

   1. For Reverse Trading System
   2. For Income Tax Harvesting

   Reverse trading is a system created by me, in which, to manage losses, we sell a stock when it falls by more than half of its recent yearly high. For example, the stock of Adani Gas reaches a 52-week high of 1,626.20 on June 11, 2021. After that, the stock falls very sharply to the level of 855 on July 19, 2021. But it came down to its 52-week high of 1,626.20, i.e., it never came down below 813.10. Before that, it started growing again and in January 2022, this stock was trading at 1,802. So, that is to say, if your stock does not fall by more than half after making its annual high, then there is a chance of its recovery anytime.

But stocks that have fallen by more than half after reaching their annual highs, their probability of recovering so quickly (2 within 1 year) is only 5 percent. For example, in the case of Yes Bank, you must have seen that if you do not keep a stop-loss and there is a loss in any stock, then you should keep an eye on the stock. As soon as the stock starts falling below half of its yearly high, sell it at once and book the capital loss or actual loss.

After that, if the stock goes down or declines further then let it go. When you feel that the stock has fallen significantly and is starts to stabilize, then buy it back. You don't understand reverse trading. Don't worry, I will explain with a simple practical example. Suppose a stock made an annual high of ₹ 100, after that it started falling and came down to 80. You bought that share at 80. Suppose you invested 8,000 by buying 100 shares at 80. Now, unfortunately, your stock starts falling further. According to reverse trading, if the annual high level of 100 falls below half of that i.e. below 50, then you have to sell the share once. Suppose you sold 100 shares at 48. Now you have got ₹ 4,800 and you booked a loss of 8,000-4,800 = 3,200. But this loss will not be like stop-loss hit. In my 17 years of stock market experience, I have seen that if the stock breaks more than half of its annual high in 90 percent of the cases, it falls even more.

Now if the stock falls further and after a few months, it becomes stable at around ₹ 25. To become stable means that if the stock continues to trade at 22-23-24-25-26 for 20 consecutive trading days, then assume that it has stabilized.

Let's say that after stabilization, you bought back 100 shares at ₹ 25 and invested 2500. So, what happened? You bought 100 shares again by putting 2,500 back out of ₹ 4,800 you had got from selling shares at 48, leaving you with 4,800-2500 = ₹ 2,300. Now the 100 shares that you had bought for 8,000 are back and ₹ 2,300 shave been left additionally. That is, now your cost of holding remains 8000-2300 = 5700 and if the share goes above 57 then you can sell and exit in profit. To understand more about this method, watch related videos by searching reverse trading on my YouTube channel Mahesh Chandra Kaushik.

Another reason to book a loss is income tax harvesting. That is, you intentionally book a loss in a stock so that you can take advantage of income tax exemption by reducing that loss from your profit. Many investors do this. After selling the share at a loss, they buy back the same share at the same time or the next day, which is considered a fresh purchase. With this, they retrieve the same number of shares at almost the same price. But they take the exemption of income tax by deducting the loss that they booked from the profit earned in that year.

I personally never book a loss to get income tax exemption intentionally nor do I advise my followers to do so. There is a reason for it. Suppose you invested 10,000 by buying 100 shares of a company at ₹ 100 and after the stock fell to 80, you booked a loss for 2,000 and bought back the shares at 80. Now you may be relieved that you have got income tax reduced on the income of 2000. But in reality, when you sell the shares bought at 80 back for 110, then this time you will have to pay tax on the income of 3,000 on the basis of profit of ₹ 30 rupees per share, whereas if you do not buy new shares by selling 100 shares at a loss, then you will have to sell them for 110. But on the basis of only ₹ 10 rupees per share, only 1,000 income would have been taxed. So, overall, things remain the same.

3. **Loss of Interest or Opportunity Loss on Capital:** If you invest in a stock today and hold it for one year and after that, you get a 4 percent profit, then in reality your profit is also a loss because if you had invested the same amount in bank FD or bonds for 1 year, you would have earned up to 6-7 percent interest, whereas you have earned only 4 percent by holding for 1 year here. So, if you see, you have lost 2-3 percent return here as compared to a bank FD or bond.

4. **Loss in Profit:** There are times when your stock rises continuously, then you don't sell it at a profit. After that the stock suddenly falls, reducing your profit to negligible or even less. Although there is no real loss to you in this case the reduction in profit looks like a loss to you. There is only one way to avoid this – keep the profit target fixed that you have to sell the shares as soon as you reach a certain percentage of profit.

Now it is time to give you information about what are the steps to avoid losses:

1. **Keep Your Portfolio Diversified:** My maths in this regard is very simple – you should not invest more than 1/33 of your total investible capital in 1 share. If your total capital is 3.30 lakhs, then do not invest more than 1/33 of 3.30 lakhs

i.e., more than ₹ 10,000 (ten thousand) in one share, and keep shares of 33 different companies in your portfolio. Now you may ask how will you take out the average? So, you had only ₹ 3.30 lakhs and if you put 10,000 in one share and keep 33 shares, then how will you take out the average? The answer is that if you want to adopt my smart average method, then you have to divide this 10,000 also into 4 parts, and the first ₹ 2500 have to be invested in 1 share. You will understand the description of this method later.

2. **Invest Only in ETFs, REITs and INVITs:** 5-10 years ago, advice was given that if you want to earn safely in the stock market, then you should invest only in blue-chip companies. Blue-chip companies means companies with high market cap, or you can consider companies included in Nifty 50 and Sensex as blue-chip. But recently, in the last 5-10 years, Yes Bank stock had fallen from ₹ 400 to ₹ 6 in the stock market and India Bulls Housing Finance fell from ₹ 1300 to ₹ 100. Similarly, PNB also saw a decline of more than 50 percent. These were all blue-chip companies with high market caps. Yes Bank was a company included in Nifty 50. In such a situation, this advice is no longer relevant that if you invest only in Nifty 50 stocks, then you will never make a loss. Therefore, now the new trend among investors is investing in ETFs, REITs, and INVITs.

   ETF means Exchange Traded Fund, which consists of many shares like mutual funds and not just one share and they trade like shares. REIT stands for Real Estate Investment Trust and INVIT stands for Infrastructure Investment Trust. They are types of property mutual funds, which are traded like shares on the exchange. So, it is safer to invest in these as the combination of many stocks (or many properties) in them does not result in a huge overall fall and they eventually recover.

3. **Invest Only in Top 10 Market Cap Companies:** Recently I received an e-mail from a professor, in which he said that he had been investing only in the top 10 companies with the highest market cap of Nifty 50 for the last 13 years. And with this, he also bought land, built a house, and also opened a coaching centre. I have shown the professor's e-mail in a video on my YouTube channel. Overall, not all blue-chip companies are secure these days. So, either invest only in ETFs or invest only in the top 10 companies of Nifty (companies with highest market cap).

4. **Use Smart Averaging Method:** First of all, before buying a share, invest only after you are certain about both that the fundamentals of the company are strong and your purchase price is reasonable. Secondly, do not invest more than 1/33 of your total capital and follow the 'Buy Right Sit Tight' formula, that is, once you buy, do not rush to book profits and if there is a fall, do not panic and if possible, do not even average after the fall. But still, if you do not want to keep the fallen stocks in your portfolio and do not want to exit even after incurring a loss, then my smart averaging method can prove to be helpful to you. Before proceeding, remember that if you want to convert loss into profit with the smart averaging method, then only invest 1/4th of the 1/33 part of the total capital that you have allocated for any share in the share for the first time. Then if the stock falls by more than 10 percent then you can reinvest the remaining 1/4.

Now if you ever get a chance to get profit after averaging, then exit. Unfortunately, if the stock falls further, then invest the remaining 1/4 of the amount after 'the fall of 20 percent of the average price'. Consider this point carefully. Here, it is not mentioned after a 20 percent fall of the first buy, here it is mentioned after a 20 percent fall in the average price.

Let me explain this to you with a practical example. Suppose Sachin Gupta is an investor. He first invests 2,500 by buying 25 shares at ₹ 100 per share. Now he wants a profit target of 3.75 percent on 2,500. (According to me, the 3.75 percent profit target is the standard target. Read my book 41 Trading Tipss for more details.) That target, i.e., 103.75 is not reached and the stock falls to ₹ 90. So, he buys 28 shares at ₹ 90 and invests 2,520. Now their average price would be 5,020/53 = 94.72 for a total of 53 shares as per investment of 5,020. Brokerage is not added here for ease of calculation. You also need to add brokerage. Now the next purchase is not to be done after falling 100 to 20 percent i.e. 80. This average price will fall by 20 percent from 94.72 i.e., at 75.78. At this price, an investment of 2500.74 will be made by taking 33 shares. Now the average price of a total of 86 shares will be 87.45. Next, if you have to average one last time, you will calculate this average when the price falls by 30 percent i.e., to a price of 61.22 from 87.45. But don't average more than that.

With this smart average, if you are investing in ETFs, Nifty Top 10, or good fundamental blue-chips, then you will get a profit in 90 percent of the cases. Otherwise, even if you want to hold for 1, 2, or 3 years, then only 1/33 part of your total capital will be held, and the remaining 32 parts will continue to earn. Even if you incur a loss, it will be less than 1/33 of the total capital.

I hope that all the above-given tips will be useful to you in dealing with losses in the stock market. The gist of all is that if you can't hold a stock for a long period of time, don't watch the prices too often even if there are ups and downs in every market. Buying or selling shares can lead to losses owing to market volatility. Do not move like the sheep. Do not invest in the market by looking at other users/investors. Invest money only when you are absolutely sure. Many investors, due to the fear of falling behind their peers, repeatedly buy and sell the wrong shares in a hurry. You should stay away from it and accept your mistakes.

No one can foresee financial crises and an investor can come face to face with financial crises at any time. In times like these, it is important to maintain restraint. These falls are the best opportunities to make money.

Loss can be avoided if you follow the advice of well-known or reputed investors in a falling stock market.

According to Warren Buffett, if there is a continuous fall in the market, then the trader or investor should be patient. In this scenario, selling the shares should be avoided. Investors should keep their basics in mind instead of selling, that is, buy shares and keep them for a long period. No one can predict when the decline will stop. So, keep a close eye on the market and take decisions with restraint instead of panicking.

Many experts say that being intimidated by a market breakout is not the right strategy. If you are a smart investor then you can find opportunities for yourself in every situation. Of course, you should take care not to lose patience. Also, don't follow other investors. If other investors are scared, then you should become greedy.

If you want to eat sweet fruits, then first of all you have to plant that tree of sweet fruit. This means investing by planning for the long term. Instead of becoming a regular trader in the market, aim for the long term. Be patient till the target is completed because the fruit of patience is sweet.

Invest money in reputable companies. For this, you can analyse those companies. This reduces the chances of a risk occurring. Most importantly, believe in yourself that you can become a smart investor.

If you can't hold a stock for long, don't even think of holding it for a day. If you have invested, do not look at its prices frequently, even if the market is fluctuating. Buying or selling shares based on the volatility in the market can lead to losses.

❑

9
Know the Delisting

"The price is what you pay. Value is what you get."

–Warren Buffett

When a listed company delists its shares from the stock exchange, it is called delisting. Typically, delisting occurs when a company ceases its operations, merges with another company, seeks to expand or reorganize, declares bankruptcy, wants to become private, or fails to meet listing requirements.

After delisting, if you have shares of that company, then you will not be able to sell them on the stock exchange and their value becomes zero for the common investor. Delisting is usually caused by the suspension of operations or due to merger or bankruptcy. But sometimes the stock exchange forcibly (involuntarily) delists the company for failing to meet the listing requirements.

So, delisting is of two types:

1. Voluntary
2. Involuntary

When the delisting is a voluntary decision, then as per SEBI rules, the company offers to buy back the shares of the investors by paying them. Although investors get paid they may have to surrender the shares at a loss if the share price has fallen. But when a company does not follow the rules and the stock exchange suspends it and forcibly delists it, then the investors lose the entire capital because they are not able to sell their shares. This is the reason why investors are advised to invest only in good blue-chip companies which have a long tech record and are consistently compliant and profitable. In a nutshell, if the stock is permanently removed from the stock exchange, it is called delisting.

Reasons for Voluntary Delisting: Some companies apply for Voluntary Delisting by using cost-benefit analysis to find that the profit they are getting from being listed publicly is low and the cost of staying listed is high. In this, investors are given the option of receiving the payment by tendering their shares to the company at a fixed price (which is usually around the average market price of 30 days) within a fixed period. Shareholders who do not surrender their shares during the period of voluntary delisting, continue to be the shareholders of the company. But due to the lack of trading of shares, it is not easy for them even if they ever want to sell. However, delisting shares can also be sold off-market to interested buyers.

Reasons for Involuntary Delisting: Some companies wilfully violate regulations or fail to meet minimum financial requirements. The exchange then forcibly delists such companies. Before involuntary delisting, the stock exchange gives time to such companies to follow the rules by issuing warning notices. But such companies are forcibly delisted if the requirements are not met within the stipulated time.

Overall, if you are greedy or avaricious in the stock market and choose companies without fundamentals for investment in the pursuit of making lucrative profits on the basis of small penny shares or hearsay, then you may lose your entire capital if your company is involuntary delisted.

Whenever the stock market is in a boom, then even some small companies that are only on paper and are without fundamentals get themselves listed one way or the other. For a few days, their prices increase rapidly and by using unethical means, small investors are lured into making big investments through tips, etc. After that, such companies deliberately stop adhering to the listing standards, due to which their trading is suspended by the exchange and the money of gullible investors is stuck.

So, in order to become a smart investor, I want to remind you once again that when you can make one crore by earning ₹ 500 20,000 times each, then instead of investing in small companies why not invest this ₹ 500 also in companies that pay good dividends so that you do not have regrets later on when a small company gets delisted.

❑

10
IPO or Initial Public Offering

"I am a better investor because I am a trader and I am a better trader because I am an investor."

–Warren Buffett

The literal meaning of the term IPO is 'Initial Public Offering'. When a private company wants to sell some percentage of its stake to outside investors like corporate entities, business entities, mutual funds, retail investors etc., then that company comes out with IPO. After the IPO, the company turns into a public company from a private company. Public companies are called so because they have to make all kinds of information public, such as financial, cash flow, profit and loss, shareholding, etc., on a quarterly or annual basis.

In an IPO, the company first files a document with SEBI, which is known as Draft Red Herring Prospectus (DRHP). SEBI gives permission for IPO after due verification and fulfilment of documents. Now you must be wondering how the 'Price Band' of IPO is decided. Some people believe that SEBI plays a pivotal role in deciding the price or price band of the IPO, but this is not true. SEBI has nothing to do with pricing. SEBI is a regulatory body, which is limited to the validity and scrutiny of the contents of the IPO prospectus. Basically, the role of deciding the price band of the IPO is played by the lead bank managers. The lead bank managers decide the IPO price. The company hires lead bank managers to fix the IPO price band and they fix the price based on the company's balance sheet, market values of competing companies, and future estimation.

Price Band in IPO

The price band is basically the threshold limit for the bidder on the IPO. This information is in the 'Red Herring Prospectus' published by the company for the IPO. The price band is the price between the 'floor price' and the 'cap price', the difference between which should not exceed 20 percent.

For example, a company 'LIC' invites applications for an IPO. Their possible price band ranges from ₹ 902 to ₹ 949. This means that your minimum bid should be ₹ 902. Failure to do so will result in your application being rejected.

The price band of an IPO tells the potential buyer about the company's price and the potential return through the IPO. By keeping the price band in mind and carrying out a comprehensive analysis of the IPO, you can decide whether you want to invest in IPO or not.

By the way, most IPO investors apply only at the highest level of the price band so that they have maximum chances of getting the shares allotted.

In my personal opinion, I don't respect the price band of IPO at all. I am also an officer in accounting services. In relation to this, let me tell you a popular joke about accountants (people from accounting services). Once a company was about to recruit some accountants for its financial accounts. The CEO of the company, after an introduction with all the potential candidates, would ask some formal questions. At the end, he would ask everyone, "How much is two and two?' Upon hearing this question, the contestants would laugh and answer. After hearing the answer, the CEO would end the interview and say, "Okay, if you are selected, the company will notify you by e-mail." Finally, a participant appeared, who when asked by the CEO, "How much is two and two?" said, "Sir, it depends on how many you want."

The CEO asked, "How?" He said, "Sir, when I work for the company, I will analyse balance sheets. and collect statistics, in the manner that you would like the answer for two and two. I can make them three and five, too." That candidate was selected. Overall, I would recommend instead of investing in IPO, investing in the company after one year of its listing, that too if the company seems worthy of investment. The following are the reasons for that:

1. The assumption that one gets the company cheaper in IPO is wrong. The price band fixed by the company in IPO is not always cheap.

2. In my 17 years of stock market experience, I have observed that 90 percent of the companies' shares start trading cheaper than the IPO price in the secondary market within 1 year of the IPO coming out.

3. Regarding investing in IPO for listing gain, most of the shares which are listed at higher prices than the issue prices are not allotted to small investors and the shares which are listed below are allotted. This makes investors feel cheated.

4. After trading for 1 year of listing, the results of 4 quarters of the stock are also revealed and the market gives the share its actual valuation. Recently Paytm's IPO came out, which was a very big IPO. In this, the issue price of the share was fixed at ₹ 2,150 per share. At the time of writing this book, it was trading at 544 in May 2022, about 6 months after the IPO. Overall, it is better not to invest in IPO and invest after waiting for 1 year. But this does not mean that there is no

profit in IPO. The shares of some companies get listed at more than the issue price and even twice or three times. But you do not have any criteria to know your valuation. You and I are small investors, we are no lead bank managers. That's why we don't get to know whose valuation is low and whose valuation is high. From the data given in the Red Herring Prospectus of IPO, the valuation of all of them seems logical. But its true valuation emerges after entering the market.

The basic purpose of the information in this chapter is that you should never think that buying in IPO makes the stock cheaper and that it will increase after that. This type of assumption is absolutely fallacious and in 90 percent of the cases, after the IPO, there is a possibility of getting the shares at a lower price in the secondary market.

❑

11
Fundamental Analysis of Company Stocks

Fundamental analysis of stocks is a method of stock valuation, in which the true value of the stock is calculated through economic analysis of the stock. Fundamental analysis of stocks gives you the basis to predict the movement of stock prices. It takes into account the financial position of a particular company as well as factors affecting the entire industry.

What is the Importance of Fundamental Analysis: Fundamental analysis is used by long-term investors, financial advisors and fund managers as they can use it to buy good stocks at low prices. At present, the share of Page Industries in the Indian market is ₹ 41,651 (February 2022). The same stock stood at ₹ 486.80 on May 30, 2008. There are many such examples. You can search for past prices of Eicher Motors, TTK Prestige etc. Based on my fundamental analysis, I publish research reports on the companies with potential for future growth once or twice a month on my blog **www.maheshkaushik.com.**

Now you are being given information about how to do the fundamental analysis of a company.

1. **Information on Liquidity Ratio:** There are two types of liquidity ratios:

(i) Current Ratio

(ii) Quick Ratio

Liquidity ratios measure the liquidity of a company at a given point in time. This gives an idea of the company's ability to convert assets into cash to pay off its liabilities if the company becomes insolvent. The current ratio is arrived at by dividing a company's current assets by its current liabilities.

Current Ratio = Current Assets / Current Liabilities

Suppose, the current assets of a company are ₹ 100 crores and liabilities are of ₹ 120 crores. So, dividing current assets ₹ 100 crores by liabilities ₹ 120 crores gives the current ratio of 0.83. This means that even after selling all the assets of the company, sufficient amount will not be generated to pay all the liabilities. Therefore, such companies, whose current ratio is less than 1, cannot be considered good for investment. Similarly, if it is reversed, i.e., assets are ₹ 120 crores and liabilities are ₹ 100 crores, then this ratio will be 120/100 = 1.20, i.e., 20 crores will be left even after paying all the liabilities. Therefore, preference is given to companies with a current ratio of more than 1. But the quick ratio is given more priority in fundamental analysis than the current ratio because the quick ratio is calculated by dividing the company's liquid assets by the liabilities. A liquid asset means an asset which can be easily sold. You can get information about the current ratio and quick ratio from websites like Money Control or from the company's annual report.

2. **Information about EPS:** The earning per share in a share is called Earning Per Share or EPS in short. Suppose, a company has a total of ₹ 20 lakhs shares and its profit (net profit) is ₹ 40 lakhs. So, dividing the profit of ₹ 40 lakhs by

the total number of shares of ₹ 20 lakhs gives the company's total EPS of ₹ 2.

3. **Valuation of the Stock by P/E Ratio:** If the part of the EPS obtained above is divided into the current market price of a stock, then its share price earnings ratio is obtained. For example, in the above example of share, if the market price of the company is ₹ 80, then its P/E ratio (Price/Eps) will be 80/2 = ₹ 40. This means now a share earns ₹ 2 per year and we buy it at ₹ 80. Then at the P/E of 40, we are buying that share by paying as much money as 40 years' earnings. Now if the income of the company does not increase, then that means that we have paid the same amount as the earnings per share of the company for 40 years when we purchased that share. Therefore, if the earnings of that stock do not increase, then there is less chance of its price going up. If we get the same share for ₹ 6, then its P/E is only 3. That is, if we buy that share only at the value of 3 years' EPS, then the chances of it increasing in the future would have been high. In short, if the P/E is high then the valuation of the stock is expensive and if the P/E is low then the valuation of the stock is low. But it also does not simply mean that you should buy the stocks of companies with low P/E without thinking and then start blaming this book.

    You should compare the P/E of similar companies in the same sector. For example, company A's P/E is 21 and company B's P/E is 14 and both the companies belong to the same sector. Now you would think that company B's valuation is cheap due to the low P/E and you should buy it. But you should also check its historical P/E (which can be found in company annual reports or on sites like Money Control). If the P/E of company A increases year after year and has increased from 18, 19, 20 to 21 and the EPS is also increasing, then the company is growing.

Company B's P/E is decreasing and from 17, 16, 15, it has come down to 14 and the EPS is also decreasing, then the company is slowly sinking and you should not board the sinking ship.

4. **Sales Per Share:** I prefer Net Sale Par Share over Earning Per Share. This is because the profit of a company can be easily shown as high/low while preparing the balance sheet, but the sale of the company is more important than its profit. Suppose, the sale of company A is ₹ 10,000 crores and the company has 100 crore shares. So, sales per share = 10,000/100 = ₹ 100. On the other hand, the sale of company B is ₹ 2000 crores and it also has 100 crore shares. So, its sale per share would be 2000/100 = ₹ 20.

   Now if company A makes a profit of 200 crores, then its EPS will be ₹ 2 per share, and if company B makes a profit of ₹ 400 crores, then its EPS will be ₹ 4 per share. Who would you prefer now? In my opinion, company A should not be given preference on the basis of higher EPS because ₹ 400 crore profit on ₹ 2000 crore sales means 20 percent profit, which is not possible to earn continuously, whereas the company's ₹ 10,000 crore sales is 5 times more than that of company B. The reason for its low profit may be that it is investing in expansion. But in the future, the effect of more sales or more market share must be reflected in his profit. Overall, you have to read the balance sheet carefully keeping all these facts in mind.

5. **Leverage Ratio:** It is also known as Debt/Equity Ratio. Debt Equity Ratio = Total Debt/Total Equity. When the debt of the company is high, then the debt-equity ratio will also be high and if the debt is low then this ratio will also be low. Very high debt is not considered advisable for a company. You can check the debt-equity ratio on websites like Money

Control or by downloading the company's annual report from NSE and BSE. It is better not to invest in companies with a debt-equity ratio of more than 1 as their leverage is high.

6. **EBITDA Margin:** If you watch business channels on television or on YouTube, then you must have heard the term EBITDA margin. It is also called the profitability ratio. This can be used to assess a business's ability to make profits. The full form of EBITDA is Earning Before Interest Taxes Depreciation and Amortization. EBITDA is the profit/ income made before deducting interest, tax, depreciation, etc. from the total gross profit. You can see this in the company's balance sheet and its quarterly results.

7. **ROE or Return on Equity:** ROE means Return on Equity. The formula for its calculation is

   ROE = (Net Profit/Equity) × 100

   So, when you want to choose between two companies in the same sector, you can compare their ROE ratio.

8. **Price to Book Value Ratio:** If the current price of a company is divided by the book value, then the price to book value ratio is obtained.

   P/BV = Market Price/Book Value

   For example, if the value of a company is ₹ 120 and its book value is 60, then the P/BV ratio will be 120/60 = 2. There is another company, whose market value is also 120, but its book value is only ₹ 1.20, so its P/BV = 120/1.20 = 100. Overall, the lower the P/BV, the higher the book value of the company, and the cheaper the stock. Here again, let me remind you that I prefer Price to Net Sell Per Share rather than Price to Book Value because Book Value can be over-represented due to depreciation etc. but Earning Per Share is such a constant that it is difficult for any company to manipulate it.

Know About the Company

Fundamental analysis of stocks requires understanding the company that you have chosen to invest in. If you have very little knowledge then you cannot judge the performance of the company. So, you should try to collect the following information, such as

- Is the company performing well or not?
- What's going on inside the company?
- What will be the impact of the change in management of the company?
- Is the company making the right decisions for its future goals?

Go to the company's home page and check everything; for example – product, business, customer, geography, mission and vision, etc.

If you are satisfied then proceed to the next step; otherwise, ignore it.

Examine the Company's Financial Reports

After knowing all about the company, you should move ahead and study the financial report of the company. Studying financial reports is one of the most crucial steps in the fundamental analysis of stocks.

Financial reports include profit and loss accounts, balance sheets and cash flow statements.

The balance sheet is reviewed to understand the financial position of the company. The income statement is used for understanding the profit or loss of a business within a given period, whereas cash flows are used to understand the cash flow as of a given period.

Annual Reports

An annual report plays the most seminal or key role in the fundamental analysis of any stock. It is filed by all public companies and contains all the important information about the company. It is published at the end of the year and includes data up to March 31. It is a large document and reading the entire annual report can be a tedious process.

Balance Sheet

The balance sheet is a way of representing the assets and liabilities of a company or a particular period. It is necessary to analyse various items to know the overall position of the company. For example, both too much debt and too little debt on the balance sheet are areas of concern. Too much debt means high financing costs and thus low profitability. Too little debt could mean the company isn't taking steps to expand itself. Thus, a perfect balance is needed everywhere.

Profit and Loss (P&L) Statement

P&L presents us with a comprehensive picture of the company's profitability. All the major components in the P&L statement can be seen on a comparative basis. For example, the revenue for the third quarter of the year 2021 should be compared with the revenue for the third quarter of 2020.

Cash Flow Statement

This statement provides a detailed report on the cash flows through various activities of the company. It gives a good idea about the liquidity or cash flow of the company predicting the profitability of the company.

Examining Company's Debt

The company's debt needs to be checked before investing. Debt is one of the biggest factors, which can change the entire future of the company. You should always avoid companies with huge debt as a company with huge debt may not reward its shareholder. Their huge debt can spoil the performance of the company.

Finding Company Peers

When you decide to invest in a company, you should first look for peers like this company and check why the company is different from its peers. What is that unique aspect that makes your selected company better than its peers?

The Unique Selling Point (USP) of a company sets it apart from its competitors. The details of upcoming projects, future prospects, new projects etc. of the selected company are given in the USP of the company. So, try to find the USP of the company with the help of the internet.

Analysing the Future

Finally, try to analyse the growth prospect of the company. If you want to invest in long-term stocks, always choose companies whose products and services will be in demand for the next 15 years or more as these parameters will help in saving the company in the long run, and ultimately, will give the investors long-term benefits.

I hope that the information given in this chapter has added to your knowledge of fundamental analysis and with the help of the above ratios, it will be easy for you to select the shares for your investment.

❑

12
Learn Technical Analysis

Every investor wants to use the best methods of stock analysis so that the method he chooses and by applying it, the selected stocks will perform best in every market situation. Unfortunately, no method of analysis in the stock market is 100 percent perfect. That's why I always recommend investors to mix different methods for stock selection instead of using a single method. Therefore, along with fundamental analysis, you must also have knowledge of technical analysis of stock because, with technical analysis, we can easily predict the short-term movement of a stock.

In technical analysis, the stock's value is predicted by studying its behaviour from the past historical data of the stock. In technical analysis, by using charts, with the help of technical indicators like volume and RSI, the stock is analysed to see the pattern of the stock in order to earn money quickly from the short-term movement. Keep in mind here that the technical analysis of a stock is not related to its (company's) fundamentals. Hence it should always be used only for making small short-term trades. Technical analysis was invented by Charles Henry Dow. That's why he is called the Father of Technical Analysis.

The Mainstay of Technical Analysis: Technical analysis assumes that the value of stock consists of all known and unknown information at that time. That's why you are asked to respect the stock price. That is, the value of a share in the stock market at a given point in time is after discounting all the known and unknown information at that time. Now you will say that this is all so confusing. Let me explain it in detail. The market started falling in October 2021, even before the Russia-Ukraine war started in February 2022. That is, the market players already knew that something like this could happen.

The same thing holds true for any stock. If any good news regarding a stock is about to appear, then the people or their acquaintances who know this news already start buying that stock, due to which its volume and price start increasing. Therefore, even before the news is out, its chart pattern signifies that something positive is going to happen in that stock.

That is, the future trend of the stock can be predicted from the price movement and volume on the chart. Technical analysis is a very broad subject, on which a separate book can be written. In this book, Technical Analysis will be briefly presented in its modern form. In technical analysis, along with using charts and graphs, indicators like Moving Average, Sport Resistance, RSI, etc. are used. There are also many types of charts—bar charts, candlestick charts, line charts, point and figure charts, etc.

Candlestick charts are commonly used because they are easy to interpret. But I use charts and graphs for their technical analysis, using their simple and modern forms, which can be easily understood and used by common investors without expensive software. Today in this book, I will explain to you a method of technical analysis; if you understand it, you will not need to learn any other method and your full money invested in buying this book will be recovered.

Actually, Technical Analysis is a very broad topic, on which a whole book can be written separately. Therefore, those who want to learn technical analysis in detail for free, they can learn technical analysis in Hindi and English with examples and charts in a very simple language for free by visiting Zerodha's Varsity app. At present, courses are available only in English on the Varsity app. But on its website, you will find lessons in Hindi also. In this book, I will explain to you my own invented technical indicator 'Super Breakout'.

With 'Super Breakout', you will get indicators for both buying and selling, which are correct in 80 to 90 percent of the cases; you already know that there is no method that is 100 percent perfect. The super breakout method is very simple. In this, we see the moving averages of 5, 10, 20, 50, 100 and 200 days of stock. You will find this moving average very easily on Money Control's website. Now if the moving average of 5, 10, 20, 50 and 100 days is less than its 200-day moving average, then whenever such a stock crosses its 200-day moving average from below, then it will become a Clear Buy and according to any technical analysis, almost all its indicators will give Buy Signal only.

Now if you understand the whole thing, then please give a 5-star review for my book because reading your review gives me great pleasure and that is my only Guru-Dakshina.

For example, on March 13, 2022, the price of a share was running at ₹ 36.25. According to the website of Money Control, all its DMAs at that time were as follows:

5 DMA = 35.38

10 DMA = 35.18

20 DMA = 36.27

50 DMA = 38.53

100 DMA = 39.47

200 DMA = 39.72

So, here is the simple assumption that whenever such stock moves above 200 DMA, it will be the start of a long bullish trend because if 200 DMA are higher and the rest of the DMA are lower, it means that the stock has fallen from the top to bottom. But if it moves back above 200 DMA, then it is a clear trend reversal.

Now, remember a few things

1. Although using this intraday trade can be taken as soon as it moves above 200 DMA. But I will advise against it because I believe that your margin can be forfeited by closing the stock down for a day if your trade is visible on the screen to big players in intraday even if it rises up the next day.
2. So, it is better to use MTF or at least 1 month's calls than intraday. In any case, calls and futures are dangerous for small investments. So, if you trade in the stock market with less than ₹ 50 lakhs then it would be better not to do call, put, or future because with less capital you will not be able to hedge well by buying and selling call puts at different levels and your chances of losing will be high.
3. It is best to buy such shares for holding with your own money and sell back with the same method only when the sell indicator comes.
4. Invest not more than 1/33 of your total investible amount in one share. Now you would wonder that though the method is good who will check so many DMAs every day out of so many 2,000 stocks. Don't worry about it. On my YouTube channel, I have put two videos of Super Breakout, in which I have taught how to make a Google Finance Sheet of these, which will automatically check which stock is meeting this criterion, which one is worth buying, and which is saleable.
5. The best thing in this super breakout is that when the buy signal comes, then you buy it in the cash market for holding with cash amount and sell only when the sell signal comes.

6. Now, let me explain to you when the sell signal will come as per this rule. Whenever the stock's 5 DMA, 10 DMA, 15 DMA, 50 DMA, 100 DMA is more than its market price and the share price crosses its 200 DMA from top to bottom, it signals the start of a downtrend for the long term. As of March 14, 2022, a company's stock was trading at 2,339, its various DMAs were as follows:

   5 DMA = 2,461.06

   10 DMA = 2,484.94

   20 DMA = 2,474.44

   50 DMA = 2,495.14

   100 DMA = 2,445.66

   200 DMA = 2,167.95

So, now if for any reason, this share goes below 2,167.95, then technically it is time to slow down or if already holding shares of such a company, then it is time to sell out. At this time, if the stock is at a profit, then it is your profit and if it is at a loss then it is your stop-loss.

Overall, you should keep in mind that it is not necessary that this technical indicator should work for intraday. But if your time frame is 1 to 3 months, then it works well in 80 to 90 percent of the cases. On my blog, you will get its automatic Google Finance Sheet, which will scan the data daily and tell you which are the stocks that have gone above 5, 10, 15, 50, 100 DMA and are now about to cross 200 DMA from bottom to top. Similarly, this sheet also informs you to sell stocks that have gone below 5, 10, 15, 50, 100 DMA and are about to cross 200 DMA from top to bottom.

One thing that should always be kept in mind regarding such stocks is that you should buy only when the stock goes above 200 DMA and sell only when the stock goes below 200 DMA. Do not rush and buy and sell as soon as it approaches the trigger point.

When the trigger point is clearly crossed, then only true breakouts are found in 80 to 90 percent of buy and sell cases. Read the rest in my book 41 Trading Tips; with that, you will also learn the art of placing the target and stop-loss.

❑

13
Best Investment Options

"Never depend on a single income, invest to create a second source."

Investors want higher returns on their investments. Many times, investors try to double their wealth even after taking a slight risk. But the truth is that with less risk, you will get higher returns. Therefore, while choosing investment options, it is necessary to assess your risk appetite because if you can take more risks, then the returns you will get will also be high.

There are two investment options

1. Investments Related to Capital Markets
2. Investing in Debt, Gold, and Real Estate apart from Capital Market

Most Indians, till now, have been investing in investment options like gold, bank FDs real estate, etc. only other than the capital market as they do not want to take risks with their investments. Therefore, in this chapter, you will be suggested other investment options other than stocks so that you can earn great returns even with less risk.

1. **Equity Mutual Funds:** You can earn returns from Equity Mutual Funds with much less risk than the risk involved in investing directly in stocks. As per SEBI guidelines, a

mutual fund that invests at least 65 percent of its portfolio in stocks is called an equity mutual fund scheme.

When you invest in shares, the entire investment made in the company becomes zero when the company goes bankrupt. But this is not the case with mutual funds because in mutual funds the fund manager invests in many different companies. When you buy one unit of a mutual fund, you buy a portion of the entire portfolio. Due to this, even if one company goes bankrupt in the entire portfolio, it has a marginal effect on you owing to the performance of other companies. So, historically equity mutual funds and ETFs have easily given 15 percent annualized returns when held for more than 5 years. If you want to know more about Equity Mutual Funds, then you can read my book How to Achieve Financial Freedom with the Miracle of SIP. In the next chapter also, you will be given detailed information about investing in mutual funds. For now, let us discuss other investment options.

2. **Debt Mutual Funds:** Debt Mutual Funds are for those investors who want guaranteed earnings from their investments. Investing in debt mutual funds for one, three or five years gives an annual return of 5, 6 or 7 to 8 percent, almost similar to bank FDs. Still, this option is better than bank FDs in many ways.

   I have started a series on my YouTube channel a small profit of 500-500 can be booked 20,000 times to create a fund of ₹ 1 crore. Maybe you are surprised. No problem. Take a calculator and multiply 20,000 by 500. The answer will be ₹ 1 crore. Under this series, I challenged the investors that I will show them a fund of ₹ 1 crore by earning from Real Trade. In this series, I add a new video every 4 months and show how far the journey of ₹ 1 crore has come. For this series, I invest half of every 500 profit that I book in my

Zerodha trading account in SBI Corporate Bonds which is a debt fund. Debt funds earn returns by investing in corporate bonds, government securities, treasury bills, commercial papers, etc. My followers keep commenting and emailing me constantly that if I invest in equity mutual funds instead of corporate bond funds (debt funds), which have 6-7 percent returns, then I will get 15 to 20 percent returns and the journey for 1 crore will be complete very soon. But this argument of my followers is wrong for the following reasons:

1. The biggest reason is that returns in equity mutual funds are not guaranteed. The 15 to 20 percent return that you see in a bull market sometimes turns negative when there is a war or recession, whereas, in debt funds, like bank FDs, 6 to 8 percent almost guaranteed return is available. You see, I put 1/2 part of the 500 that I earn directly from shares in this fund and keep the remaining 1/2 part for income tax, growth of trading account and personal use. In this way, putting the earnings of the shares back in the equity fund will be a double risk, i.e., if there is a recession, then the investment of the shares will be stuck for a long time. But if their earnings remain in debt and not in equity funds, then the equilibrium will be maintained and you will be able to withdraw from debt funds if needed during a recession.

2. The second reason is that if I had kept this money in a bank FD, I would have to pay income tax again to the government on the interest earned from it, which according to my income would have been around 35 percent including 30 percent income tax and surcharge, cess, etc. That means I would have to pay income tax again after getting the FD with the money that I saved by paying income tax, whereas in corporate bond funds, till the time I do not book profits (for 10 or 20 years),

income tax will not be charged. Secondly, whenever I book profit, I will get the benefit of indexing i.e., if any return is left after adjusting the inflation rate, then I will have to pay income tax on that amount only, which will be less or zero.

3. Third, banks are continuously reducing the interest rate. In foreign countries, the interest rate has become zero, or in some countries, it is minus, which means the bank charges you for the security of your money and does give you interest. In such a situation, if the interest rates are further lowered, then the returns on these funds will be far ahead of bank FDs.

4. On breaking the bank FD before the term end, the bank charges a penalty or gives less interest than the fixed rate. But by getting returns on the basis of NAV in it, it gives growth on a daily basis and whenever the NAV increases on selling the units, you will get the same return and can also sell in debt funds. Now you must have understood why one should invest in debt funds apart from bank FDs and equity mutual funds.

3. **National Pension System:** You must have heard of the National Pension System or NPS. But you think that all these are useless investments. You must be wondering since no money will be available through it before 60 years, why should you block the money by investing for such a long time? But after reading this book today, your perspective about it is going to change completely. NPS was established in 2003. But it was not very popular at that time. But today common investors also prefer to invest in NPS and currently in 2022, there are about 1.5 crore subscribers of NPS. The AUM of NPS Tier-1 account has been around 6 lakh crores.

The reason for this is that NPS is a composite form of investment in shares, FDs, corporate bonds, liquid funds, government securities, etc. So, by investing in NPS, you can get the benefits of investing in all of them. So far, the annualized returns of NPS have been in the range of 9 to 12 percent, which is an admirable return considering the current interest rates. Two types of accounts can be opened in NPS:

(1) Tier-1

(2) Tier-2

(1) If the amount deposited in Tier-1 account is less than ₹ 5 lakhs upon attaining the age of 60 years, then you can withdraw the entire amount. But if the total fund amount exceeds ₹ 5 lakhs, then you can take 60 percent of the amount in cash. Of the remaining 40 percent, you will have to buy a pension plan, from which you will get a monthly pension for life.

Investing in NPS provides income tax benefits. On investing in this, you currently get a rebate of up to ₹ 1.50 lakhs under Section 80C of the Income Tax Act. But under Section 80 CCD (1B), an additional exemption of up to 50,000 is also available. That is, if you want to take the benefit of more than the exemption limit of ₹ 1.50 lakhs under 80C, then investment in NPS can also get an exemption of 50,000 in addition to the limit of ₹ 1.50 lakhs. Withdrawals of less than ₹ 5 lakhs from Tier-1 to 60 years of age are completely tax-free. For the amount over 5 lakhs, 60 percent withdrawal is tax-free and it is mandatory to buy a pension plan of 40 percent.

(2) You can withdraw the amount deposited in Tier-2 anytime like an open-end mutual fund. But the investment made in it is not exempt from income tax.

4. **Senior Citizen Saving Scheme:** It can be opened in both post offices and banks. In this, interest is given at the rate of 7.40 percent per annum. If this interest is not withdrawn by the account holder, then interest on interest is not available in it. This account can be opened with a minimum of ₹ 1,000. But in this, you can deposit a maximum of ₹ 15 lakhs only. The amount deposited in this is exempt from tax under Section 80C of the Income Tax Act. But the interest on it is not tax-free. TDS is also deducted on interest if the interest income is more than ₹ 40,000 per annum. To open this account, one must be at least 60 years of age and retired army personnel should be at least 55 years of age.

5. **RBI's Taxable Bonds:** Any person in any age group can invest in them. These bonds are available with a face value of ₹ 1,000, i.e., the minimum investment that can be made in these bonds is ₹ 1,000 and there is no maximum investment limit. Interest is earned on them at the rate of 7.15 per annum. Interest is paid every 6 months. Their shortcoming is that neither is there tax exemption up to ₹ 1.50 lakhs on the investment in them under Section 80C nor is their interest tax-free. You can buy these Bonds and Treasury Bills, Sovereign Gold Bonds, etc. directly from RBI. For this, go to the website of RBI DIRECT, Rbiretaildirect.org. in.

6. **Investment in Sovereign Gold Bonds:** The Reserve Bank of India issues Sovereign Gold Bonds every month on behalf of the Government of India. These gold bonds are issued at a face value equivalent to 1 gram of gold. In these, the price is equal to 1 gram of gold. But their biggest feature is that the Government of India also gives you 2.5 percent interest annually on them. Remember a proverb about this – 'Killing two birds with one stone'. This means that if the value of gold increases after investing in sovereign gold bonds, then the value of these bonds also increases. But even if the

value does not increase, the interest is still paid on it by the Government of India at the rate of 2.5 percent annually.

The interest keeps getting credited to the bank account linked to your Demat account on a half-yearly basis.

You can buy Sovereign Gold Bonds directly through RBI. When the issue is opened, the issue of Sovereign Gold Bonds also appears on your broker's website, just like the issue of IPO.

There are 6 major advantages of investing in Sovereign Gold Bonds:

1. As it is issued by the Government of India, this investment is safer than other private bonds because the investment in it is guaranteed by the Government of India.
2. With the increase in the price of gold, the price of the bond also increases and the bond is of 8 years duration. After 8 years you get paid at the current price of gold. One bond is equal to 1 gram of gold. You can also receive payment according to the market price of gold before 8 years as these bonds are traded like shares on the NSE website. Therefore, you can sell them like shares at the current market price (which is almost equal to the current price of gold) at any time.
3. Your investment also gives a return of 2.5 percent per annum, which is not less considering the present time (in 2022 when this book was written) because at present you get a 3 percent return in your savings account and 5-6 percent in a bank FD. In comparison, this return is not less because in this you get the benefit of an increase in the value of gold along with 2.5 percent interest.
4. Capital gains acquired in this maturity are exempt from Income Tax as per the extant rules. At present, if you

hold Sovereign Gold Bonds till maturity and take returns on the increase in the value of gold after 8 years, then your income is tax-free. If you buy Sovereign Gold Bonds through trading in the secondary market rather than an outright issue, your income is subject to long-term capital gains tax after getting indexation benefit, which is negligible as indexation benefit is available.

5. If you buy gold and keep it at home, then there is a fear of it being stolen, but you can hold the sovereign gold bond in the Demat account.

6. Margin can be obtained on these bonds by pledging them with your broker as collateral. With this margin, you can trade in shares. If you hold sovereign gold bonds equal to the minimum lot size of gold in options trading, you can safely earn a monthly income by writing covered calls of gold options.

   If you want to know more about options trading, and writing covered calls, you can read my book How to Plant a Money Tree with Options Trading.

   Apart from this, loans of about 80 percent of their value can also be obtained from banks by pledging them to banks. Like stocks, Sovereign Gold Bonds are also traded on the NSE.

7. **Investing in Real Estate:** Since childhood, you must have seen that the prices of land keep increasing all the time. You must have also seen such people around you, who sold their ancestral property or who had once invested in a plot, flat, house, or shop and became rich by selling it. In fact, as the name real estate suggests, it is 'real wealth' because everything can be created. Cereals and pulses can be cultivated, and goods can be produced in factories, but land cannot be produced. The amount of land is always the same. Therefore, as the population increases, so does the

need for land. With the rise in income and development, the demand for land also increases because people prefer to live in bigger houses and they also need land for setting up industries and businesses. That's why people always assume that if they invest in real estate, they are bound to get profits in the long run.

Now you will say that investing in real estate requires lakhs of rupees and where do I get lakhs of rupees? No problem. In this book I am going to tell you the way whereby you can invest in real estate starting from just ₹ 60. For this you have to invest in REITs. The full form of REIT is Real Estate Investment Trust. That means, it is a type of mutual fund, which invests in real estate properties.

The concept of REIT is new in India, but the first REIT in America was introduced in the year 1960. The basic principle behind REITs is to allow investors to invest like stocks in a diversified portfolio of income-generating real estate properties. The first REIT was launched in America in 1960. After that REITs were so successful that as of 2022, REITs established in 39 countries of the world function successfully.

In India too, in the year 2022, three REITs are listed and they trade like shares in the stock market. They are as follows:

1. Embassy Office Parks REIT
2. Brookfield India Real Estate Trust REIT
3. Mindspace Business Parks REIT

You can buy and sell them like shares on NSE and BSE. In April 2021, their market price was ₹ 372, 314, and 347 respectively, i.e., you can buy their 1 share by investing around ₹ 340 to 380. Not only can you earn capital gains by buying and selling them like shares, but they also distribute income like dividends to their unit holders, which is very attractive.

SEBI has put in place rules under which these trusts are required to invest 80 percent of their portfolio in such assets which have been completed and from which rental income is received. Along with this, SEBI also has a rule that these trusts have to distribute 90 percent of their income among their unit holders. For example, Embassy Office Parks, which was India's first REIT, distributed income (as dividends) of around ₹ 350 on these units each in the financial year 2021-22 as follows:

1. Interest as on May 6, 2021, ₹ 1.24, Return on Capital ₹ 2.15, Dividend ₹ 2.21 per unit, taking the total to ₹ 5.60 per unit.
2. Interest as on August 4, 2021, ₹ 1.13, Return on Capital Rs. 2 per unit, Dividend ₹ 2.51 per unit, taking the total to ₹ 5.64 per unit.
3. Interest as on November 9, 2021, ₹ 1.14, Return on Capital Rs. 1.98, Dividend ₹ 2.54 per unit, taking the total to ₹ 5. 66 per unit.
4. Interest as on February 4, 2022, Rs. 0.18, Return on Capital ₹ 1.77, Dividend ₹ 2.55 per unit, taking the total to ₹ 5.20 per unit.

   That is, if I had bought about 1 unit of Embassy Office Parks REIT for ₹ 350, I would have earned an income of ₹ 22.10 in a year in 2021-22.

   I cannot build and rent a house for ₹ 350, but I can earn ₹ 22.10 in a year by buying a REIT unit for ₹ 350. That means, on an investment of 350, I received a rent of about ₹ 1.84 for the month. Thus, as the valuation of the company's assets in real estate along with regular income increases over time, I will continue to receive the same as the share price increases. Don't be greedy. Do not invest too much in them at once. Invest a small amount in all three REITs from the monthly SIP and if any other REIT gets listed in the future, then invest little by little from monthly SIP in that, too. This will gradually build up your entire portfolio of income-generating real estate in the future.

8. **Investing in Infrastructure:** Just as you can easily invest in real estate through REIT sitting at home with a small amount, you can invest in infrastructure projects like highways, roads, pipelines, warehouses, power plants etc. through INVIT. You can earn regular dividends as well as capital accretion in the long run.

Apart from 3 REITs in India, 3 INVITs are also registered with SEBI and listed on the stock market. This is also a type of mutual fund, which trades like shares and you will be surprised to know that you can start investing by buying a unit of a certain INVIT for just ₹ 50 to 60. These three listed INVITs are as follows-

(1) IRB INVIT FUND (IRBINVIT)

(2) Powergrid Infrastructure Investment Trust (PGINVIT)

(3) India Grid Trust (INDI GRID)

There is a total of 15 SEBI registered INVITs in India, out of which only three are listed on the stock market so far. This means that in the future, more REITs and INVITs will be listed on the stock exchanges in India. There is a discussion going on to make rules to include them in the indices of NSE and BSE.

Now let me give you information about the market price of these INVITs as of April 2022 and the dividend and other income distributed by them during the last year.

1. **IRB INVIT Fund:** Its 1 share (actually 1 unit) was available at ₹ 52.80 (in April 2022). In the year 2021-22, it distributed

a total income of ₹ 6.50 among its investors thrice a year in May-August-October.

2. **India Grid Trust:** It was trading at ₹ 149.37 in April 2022 and distributed income of ₹ 9.47 per unit to its investors in the year 2021-22.

3. **POWERGRID Infrastructure Investment Trust:** This is a government INVIT company. Its 1 unit was trading at ₹ 134 in April 2022 and in 2021-22 it distributed income of ₹ 4.50 per unit to the investors.

The overall gist is that some investment options are linked to the stock market and some are linked to fixed interest. You should expect the returns according to your ability to take the risk. Making money is hard, but it can be done easily by walking in the right direction. Every small step taken by you in this direction becomes important in the future.

You should start saving early in your life. This gives you an opportunity to increase your savings. You should invest from time to time or periodically by spending as little as possible while increasing the sources of income.

One should not rush in the matter of investment. Investment decisions should be made carefully. It should be started as soon as possible. You have to devote time to understanding the ways of saving, spending, budgeting, and investing.

Give two hours a week to know the investment funds. By doing this, gradually your understanding will develop. Then you will be able to make the right decisions.

Good financial planning creates avenues for achieving life goals. The most important factor in this is how much investment will be required to achieve a goal.

Employees' Provident Fund (EPF) is fine. But apart from this, if your company is offering NPS or any other savings scheme, then you should opt for it. Experts say that saving for retirement leaves you with less money in the present, but it secures your future.

Investing in equities tends to be slightly volatile in the short term, but it is best suited for the long term. It gives the highest return over the long term as compared to any asset class. You can make good money in the long run through mutual funds or by investing directly in stocks.

❑

14
How to Earn from Mutual Funds?

"By forecasting the direction of the stock market, you can never know exactly whether the stock is going to grow or not, but one definitely gets to know about the person who forecasts regularly whether he has the understanding about the stock market or not."

–Warren Buffett

The meaning of this statement is that no one can accurately predict whether the market will go up or down. Those who make such guesses can often be wrong. That's why the people who invest regularly in mutual funds always win. All over the world, investing in mutual funds through SIP is considered the safest and most rewarding.

Because there is no market forecast involved in this and no matter what the market is, you just have to invest little by little regularly. I have written a whole book on this titled – How to Get Financial Freedom with the Miracle of SIP. You can read it if you want. But here in this book, I will not disappoint you. Here also I will introduce you to my latest I-5 method of earning from mutual funds, apart from my earlier book, so that you will feel the investment made in this book is worthwhile and you will also give a 5-star rating to this book making me aware of your affection.

But before proceeding further, let me make you aware of the latest reforms implemented in the mutual fund industry so that you can get an idea of why investors are increasingly taking an interest in investing through mutual funds these days. Before the year 2008, investors used to believe that mutual funds were the safest way to invest without risk. That was why investors invested heavily in equity funds. There was also some mis-selling, in which insurance companies began selling their unit-linked insurance plans as equity mutual funds. At that time, entry load and exit load were also charged in mutual funds.

The entry load was also very high, which the distributors received in the form of commission. Mutual fund companies paid a certain percentage on selling units as exit load. This started such a vicious cycle that distributors advised investors to sell old schemes and invest in new schemes so that maximum entry load and exit load could be earned.

Due to this, investors used to get fewer units. On account of the sudden recession in 2008, when investors saw their portfolios had a 30 to 50 percent loss, they panicked and sold their mutual funds at a loss by paying an exit load. When the market is bullish, the mutual fund companies keep coming up with similar schemes with different names. But the common investor gets confused as to which scheme to invest in and which not to invest in. Therefore, after 2008, SEBI implemented the following reforms for mutual funds:

1. **Restriction on Entry Load:** This reduced the commission of distributors and investors started getting more units on their investment.

2. **Implementation of Uniform Fact Sheet:** SEBI has introduced a Uniform Fact Sheet, which has made it mandatory for the investors to disclose all the facts related to the sector and risk etc. while reporting the scheme.

3. **Implementation of Risk Meter:** After 2013, SEBI made it mandatory to categorize each scheme into low-risk, medium-risk and high-risk levels so that investors would know the level of risk involved in investing in that scheme.

4. **Registration of Investment Advisors:** SEBI started registration of Investment Advisors by fixing their eligibility and other criteria, due to which the registered Investment Advisors gave proper investment advice to the investors.

5. **Launching of Direct Plans:** Mutual fund companies have started direct plans for the investors due to the closure of entry load, in which more units are available for investing in these plans because of no commission for the distributors.

6. **Launch of Index Funds:** This is the biggest development and, in this chapter, where I am going to tell you about the earning strategy from investing in mutual funds, index funds are going to be used.

In fact, there is an old saying in the stock market that if you can't win the index, stick with the index. For example, in January 2020 the Nifty was at 12,000 and in April 2022 the Nifty is at 18,000. That is, if you had invested in Nifty in January 2020, you would have earned a 50 percent return by April 2022. So, if you trade/invest directly in stocks and in 2 years you have not achieved more than 50 percent growth, then you are not winning the index.

Therefore, the biggest advantage of investing in index funds is that in managing your portfolio, the fund manager does not have to buy and sell shares as per his/her thinking. Investing in index funds is a kind of passive investment. In this, the fund manager has to buy the same shares, which are part of the index, and buy in the same proportion in which they are part of the index.

At present, there are many index funds available in the market in India, which are based on different indices like Nifty Small Cap 250, BSE 500 etc. As I promised you at the beginning of the chapter, in this chapter, I will show you a method of investing in mutual funds so that you can get three benefits at once.

1. Regular Income
2. Advantages of Compounding
3. Safe Investment with SIP

In this one method, I have included all three processes. Every investor wants such a method of investing in mutual funds that he can earn income from profit booking from time to time. The investor also wants that his profit booking should not affect the compounding of his money and that his invested amount should increase over time by giving him compound returns in the long term.

Thirdly, the investor wants to get the benefit of Dollar-Cost Averaging from SIP. That is, instead of investing in the market at a time, he should be able to invest regularly every month so that he can get more units when the market falls and by averaging, his investment will be back in profit when the market rises again. So, in this method, I have described the 3-in-1 method. It is called the Intelligent Investor Investment in Index (IIII) or I-5 method, as the name of this book suggests.

This I-5 method is very simple and gives regular income in increasing order. One who understands this method can earn a regular monthly income consistently with the help of index mutual funds in the stock market with minimum risk. I will also explain the theoretical part of this method in this book as well as the practical data of 2.25 years from January 1, 2020 to March 31, 2022 with examples so that you can assimilate this method well.

This chapter is the heart of the book. I have invested a lot of my valuable time and hard work in the research I-5 described in this. So, read the next few pages very carefully. In short, the I-5 method is as follows:

1. Select a good mutual fund or ETF for investment based on the Nifty 50 index. ETFs are also a type of mutual fund that trades like shares on an exchange. My daughter Monica Kaushik also uses this method. For this, on my advice, she selected NiftyBees, the most traded ETF of Nifty 50. If you want, you can choose any Nifty 50 based ETF or Index fund. In this book, we will understand the practical example of the I-5 method, wherein we will use NiftyBees as it is the most traded Nifty-based ETF at present.

2. Select the lumpsum amount for initial investment, such as 2,40,000 or 1,20,000 or 60,000 or 30,000, as per your capacity or ability. But this amount should be your own (not borrowed) and you should not have a need for it for a long time (at least 10 years). So, it should not happen that your total savings is 4,80,000 and you end up choosing the entire amount in enthusiasm. Because if you do so, what will you do if you need the money? My advice is whether the amount is 9,60,000, 4,80,000, 2,40,000, 1,20,000, 60,000 or 30,000, it should be such that if you have to keep the principal amount invested for a long time, you should be free to do so.

3. It is most ideal to have a separate savings account and a separate Demat or trading account for this method so that you can balance the amount and investment. However, you can start with any Demat or savings account.

4. In the example that I will give, we will choose 1,20,000 as the starting amount. You can choose any amount in multiples of 30,000. In my opinion, if you have less than 30,000 to invest in this method, then first start saving 10 percent of your income regularly and start this method after saving at least ₹ 30,000. If you have more capital then you can start with ₹ 6 lakhs, ₹ 9 lakhs, ₹ 30 lakhs, ₹ 60 lakhs also. In this book, the initial investment of 1,20,000 will be taken as an example for explanation. Now with whatever capital you start, add or subtract in the same proportion.

5. Now let us include theory as well as practical examples so that the subject matter is not expanded much. As is my writing style, I explain the real calculations of the stock market by giving examples of imaginary persons so that the readers remain interested. Those who have read my other books will be familiar with their characters like Mohd. Abdul Aziz, Chandu, Vicky, Ghisu Bhai etc.

Our fictional character in this book is Mona. Mona is a B.Ed. student. She spends an appreciable amount of time commuting to college daily and preparing for her B.Ed. projects etc. Mona has the habit of saving since childhood. Whatever pocket money her parents used to give her, she would save it. As she has been saving since childhood, there are ₹ 1.20 lakhs in Mona's account. In December 2019, when the Nifty was at its all-time high of around ₹ 12,000, Mona developed an interest in investing in the stock market. Mona came to me for advice as to which stocks to invest in.

Her classmates had told her about some stocks that paid great returns, which were mostly ex-penny stocks. They had multiplied many times over and over again on the circuit and Mona was very excited about them. If I had encouraged her to invest in those stocks at that time, Mona's ₹ 1.20 lakhs would have come down to 15 to 18 thousand as after the arrival of Corona, they had fallen so badly that most of them had broken 80 to 90 percent.

I always face this dilemma. Whenever the stock market falls and it falls continuously, then no one comes to me asking for advice for opening a new Demat account, making new investments, buying new shares, or starting a new SIP. But when the market goes up swiftly and the time of its fall is very near, then my co-workers, my relatives, my friends, the shopkeepers in the market near me, the tempo drivers, the carpenters, masons and artisans who work in my house, the barber at my hair dressers, etc. suggest that I should take out time to help them open a Demat account or give them important tips about stock or recommend which mutual funds they should invest in.

I have written a poem on my dilemma, read it first. I don't intend to bore you. My aim is that the poem should make you understand about what is the right time to invest in the market and the right art of investing.

तेजी में इन्वेस्ट सब करें, मंदी में करे न कोय,
जो मंदी में इन्वेस्ट करे, सदा करे एंजॉय॥
तेजी-मंदी दोनों चले, तभी मार्किट कहलाय,
तेजी में बेचे न कोय, मंदी आए घबराय॥
आलसी, लालची और ऋणी, इस मार्केट में ना आय,
काबू रहे न खुद पर, मार्केट पे दोष लगाय॥
बिजनेस न्यूज सुन-सुन के, पंडित भया न कोय,
सब्र और समझ से काम ले, वही खिलाड़ी होय॥
बॉटम-बॉटम सब कहें, बॉटम बना न कोय,
जब असल में बॉटम आए, रोकड़ा बचा न होय॥
गिरता निफ्टी देखकर, महेश कौशिक दिया रोय,
बुल बीअर के बीच में फॉलोवर बचा न कोय॥

So, overall, I acted wisely and convinced Mona to invest in it after explaining the advantages of the I-5 method. Now she had to invest ` 10,000 in NiftyBees ETF every month from January 1, 2020. The balance amount lay in her savings account, for which I advised her to apply to her bank for starting the auto sweep facility. If you have Internet Banking then you can also activate Auto Sweep or MOD facility on your own through Internet Banking. Some banks call it Auto Sweep, some banks call it MOD (Multi Option Deposit) and some call it MOD Super Saving Account.

In this, the balance above 50,000 in your savings account at the end of the month will become an automatic FD of 1,000 each and if you withdraw money when you need it, then automatically this FD of 1,000 will be broken and the amount needed will be deposited in your account. If your FD breaks prematurely, then after the deduction of 1 percent penalty from the interest payable on it, the remaining interest will also be deposited in the account immediately. So, Mona has ₹ 1.20 lakhs in her savings account and she gets the MOD activated. She invests ₹ 10,094.76 by buying 78 units at NiftyBees' closing price of 129.42 on January 1, 2020. Here brokerage is ignored, later we will reduce the brokerage amount by 1 percent while selling. Now the status in Mona's account as on January 2, 2020:

1. 1 year FD in MOD = 70,000
2. Cash = 39,905-24
3. NiftyBees 78 Units

I advised Mona to focus on her B.Ed. studies, projects, and academic activities and keep investing ₹ 10,000 in NiftyBees in the same manner at the close price on the first of every month. Mona asked, 'What if I lose my ETF?' I explained that risk is associated with everything in life. You go to college by bus every day. Will you stop sitting in the bus thinking what if the bus has an accident?

Therefore, you are also advised that your investment in the stock market is always risky. I have given the example of NiftyBees here which does not mean that I am advising you to invest in the same. You can invest in SBI Nifty, ETFs or other ETFs at your discretion; there is risk with everyone. That's why I had said that you should not invest the entire capital at one go in your excitement. Only invest the amount of loss which you will be able to bear.

Now you will ask, why I had Mona's entire capital invested? The answer is that Mona's capital is actually the wealth of her parents and her father is a highly placed officer. According to her wealth, even if Mona's investment sinks, they can bear it. Then Mona asked, "When should I book profit? You said that through this, I will continue to get a monthly income in growing order throughout my life. How will I get that?"

I explained that till her holding of Nifty ETF turns out to be more than 8 per cent profit, she has to continue with the SIP of ` 10,000 per month in Nifty ETF. Only after that, we will book profit and monthly income will also start only after the first profit is booked. Here in this method, why the target of booking profit was kept at 8 percent, and why it was not more or less than that? If you also have the above question, then the answer is that the average inflation rate in the last 10 years has been around 6 percent per annum. The base rate of India's largest public sector bank is 7.55 percent.

That is, the maximum rate of interest on an FD in the bank is 7.55 percent. So, if we are able to book 8 percent profit even once in a year, then our return will be more than the bank FD and inflation rate. Also, if we book profit twice a year, then there will be a return of 16 percent. That's why I have set a profit target of 8 percent. I have not kept more than that because then it would become difficult to achieve the target. If more than 12 months elapse in waiting for the target, then your money would be exhausted, due to which you would not be able to continue the SIP further.

According to me, the profit target of 8 percent is the best target for the Nifty ETF and it is likely to keep the target of 8 percent 2-3-4 times in a year. What after that? I will explain further what you have to do after achieving the target of 8 percent. First, let's see what happened next. On February 1, 2020, Mona bought 81 more units of NiftyBees by investing 10,101.51 before the market closed around NiftyBees' closing price of 124.71. Till now her total investment was ` 20,196.27. You will remember that last month she invested at 129.42. Now the price has fallen to 124.71 and she is currently incurring a loss of ` 367.38 on her investment. No problem. She has to continue investing around ` 10,000 per month till she starts making a profit above 8 percent.

On March 2, she again bought 85 more units by investing ₹ 10,063.15. The closing price of NiftyBees on March 2, 2020 was 118.39 (The market was closed on March 1, 2020. So, the investment for March was made on March 2, 2020). Now, she was incurring a loss of 4.53 percent on her investment. Let me directly show you the status of her balance sheet as on March, 31, 2020 as she also received simple interest on the amount kept in her savings account as of March, 31,2020 at the then prevailing rate of 3.50 percent. Mona's investment status as on March 31,2020—

1. NiftyBees total 244 Units and investment in NiftyBees was (78+81+85) 30,259.42.
2. The 1-year FD in the MOD still stands at 70,000, which was already done on January 1, 2020. At that time, the interest on 1 year's FD was 6.50 percent, which will be available only after 1 year or if the FD is broken.
3. Out of the ₹ 1,20,000 in the savings account, there was a balance of 50,000 after making an FD of 70,000. There should have been a balance of 19,740.58 in the savings account after moving 30,259.42 to NiftyBees. However, the interest accrued on a quarterly basis is deposited in the savings account. At the rate of 3.5 percent per annum, her interest for 3 months came to ₹ 253.70. So, now the balance in the savings account remains 19,994.28.

Now I will not engage you in too many calculations. Let me directly tell you the status of July 21, 2020. By then, Mona had accumulated 645 units of NiftyBees, which at the close price on July 21, 2020, had come into a profit of 8.49 percent as follows:

Date	Close Price	Units Bought
January 1, 2020	129.42	78
February 1, 2020	124.71	81
March 2, 2020	118.39	85
April 1, 2020	89.35	112
May 4, 2020	98.8	102
June 1, 2020	104.42	96
July 1, 2020	90.05	91
Total Units		645

₹ 70,473.18 were invested in buying these 645 units. Since the cash in the savings account was only 50,000, the rest was auto sweep FD, out of which the FD of ₹ 21,000 was automatically broken and deposited in the cash account. At the time the FD of ₹ 21,000 was broken, after the deduction of 1 percent penalty for prepayment, the remaining interest was also deposited in her account. Do not pay much attention to how much interest you got here and what was its calculation.

Here my purpose is just to tell you that the cash which is not used in this method will also earn 5-6 percent per annum. The average price of 645 units that Mona had bought so far in 7 months was 109.26 and the closing price on July 21, 2020 was 118.54. That means Mona's investment of 70,473.18 earned a profit of 8.49 percent profit which means a profit of ₹ 5,985.12.

Now the next step of this method starts. Now Mona will start getting a regular monthly income, which will be in increasing order, and she will also get the benefit of compounding on her investment. Now Mona has to sell all the units and book a profit of ₹ 5,985.12. If you wish you can assume that out of this amount, ₹ 185.12 brokerage expenses were deducted and the net profit was ₹ 5,800 only. Now all the cash has been deposited in Mona's account, which is as follows:

1. FD in Auto-sweep = 49,000

(Out of the FD of 70,000, 21,000 was broken prematurely, which will now go back to the FD at the end of the month.)

2. Interest received in savings account on March 31 and June 30 = 400 (approximately)

3. Partial interest on the premature break-up of FD = 475 (approximately)

4. Earnings after deducting brokerage on NiftyBees = 5,800 (approximately)

5. Price Amount on Selling NiftyBees = 70,473 (approximately)

Total = 1,26,148

Now I suggested to Mona that she can withdraw ₹ 600 rupees as a monthly income from this account i.e. 0.50 percent of the initial investment of ₹ 1,20,000 to start her monthly income. If you have invested 30,000, then the monthly income of 150 has to be withdrawn. If you have invested 2,40,000, then you have to withdraw 1,200. Now from the very next day, i.e., from July 23, 2020, she has to increase SIP in NiftyBees by 5 percent again. That is, where she earlier deposited 10,000 per month in NiftyBees, now she has to deposit 10,500 per month. After each profit booking, the SIP amount has to be increased by 5 percent. For example, if Mona books one more profit, then she has to increase the next SIP of 10,500 by 5 percent to 11,025 and after each profit booking, the monthly income also has to increase by 5 percent. For example, after booking the next profit, it has to be withdrawn from the account as regular income at 630 per month instead of 600 per month. See Mona's progress over the next few months:

Date	Close Price	Units Bought	Investment
July 23. 2020	119.08	89	10,598.12
August 24,2020	122	87	10,614.00
September 23,2020	118.95	89	10,586.55
October 23,2020	127.11	83	10,550.13
Total Units and Investment		350	42,348.80

Now on November 9, 2020, her investment again closed with a profit of 9.70 percent (profit was 7.95 percent on November 6, then it closed at 9.70 percent on November 7). So, she booked a profit again and made a profit of ₹ 4,106.70. You can assume the net profit as 4,000 after deducting 106.70 as brokerage, etc. During these 4 months, Mona also took a monthly income of ₹ 2400 at the rate of ₹ 600 per month. Now after booking the profit again, the next SIP has to be increased by 5 percent (increased by 5 percent from 10,500) to ₹ 11,025. Booking profit once means that your monthly income has increased by 5 percent. Now she has to withdraw 630 instead of 600 as monthly income.

If Mona continues this system and books a profit for a total of 20 times, then her monthly income and SIP will continue to increase as follows:

Sl. No.	Profit Booking	SIP Per Month	Monthly Income
1	Initial Investment	10,000	0
2	After booking first profit	10,500	600
3	After booking second profit	11,025	630
4	After booking third profit	11,576	662

5	After booking fourth profit	12,155	695
6	After booking fifth profit	12,763	729
7	After booking sixth profit	13,401	766
8	After booking seventh profit	14,071	804
9	After booking eighth profit	14,775	844
10	After booking ninth profit	15,513	886
11	After booking tenth profit	16,289	931
12	After booking eleventh profit	17,103	977
13	After booking twelfth profit	17,959	1,026
14	After booking thirteenth profit	18,856	1,078
15	After booking fourteenth profit	19,799	1,131
16	After booking fifteenth profit	20,789	1,247
17	After booking sixteenth profit	21,829	1,310
18	After booking seventeenth profit	22,920	1,375
19	After booking eighteenth profit	24,066	1,444
20	After booking nineteenth profit	25,720	1,516
21	After booking twentieth profit	26,533	1,592

Please note - this is not the position after 20 years. This is the position after booking profit 20 times. Today if you are able to book profit 3 times in a year on an average, then this situation will come in 6-7 years. Now you would like to ask a question - what if the market keeps falling for more than 12 months and my profit is not booked even after I have exhausted all my money?

The answer is that when you invest through SIP, the chances are less that even a 12-month SIP will not book an 8 percent profit. Nevertheless, the stock market is always risky and uncertain. If that happens, lend yourself some money. I had already said that do not get too excited and do not invest your entire capital in it. Suppose that in a severe recession, you are able to take 8 percent profit by investing 16 instalments. So, after the profit is booked, you can take back the amount in 4 instalments which you had lent yourself. If this ever happens, you can imagine what will happen to the rest of the people who are use other methods instead of I-5? You will still win compared to others. Even if you ever have to book a loss, you will have withdrawn so much monthly income that it will not be a loss. The market is anyway risky and uncertain. The overall gist is that in the I-5 method, one can invest in Nifty ETFs or mutual funds through SIP.

1. You book a profit if it is more than 8 percent.

2. You do the next SIP with 5 percent more.

3. After you book the first profit, you start earning a monthly income of 0.5 percent of the amount of the first investment, which keeps on increasing by 5 percent each profit booking.

4. You will find this method boring. You also have to invest in it patiently and continuously. But believe me, this is a relatively safe and regular income-generating method of investing in the stock market.

If you liked this method, then review the book on Amazon and let me know in the comments. I will be very happy and I will consider my hard work successful.

❑

15
Earning from Commodity Trading

"It's hard to be smarter than your foolish competitor in the commodity business."

–Warren Buffett

Online commodity trading has also started in India. Retail investors have also started investing in commodities online. But like other forms of trading, in commodities also you need perseverance, knowledge, experience, and dedication. Hence the above quote, which reads – "It is very difficult to be smarter than your foolish competitor in the commodity business." Actually, who you think is a foolish competitor is a person doing business for many generations. He has experience of this business for generations.

Now you will say that 'I have not understood anything.' Actually, online trading of commodities is not meant for the common small investor. It has been created to provide online trading opportunities to those wholesalers who have worked for generations in the commodity trade. For example, there is a prominent jeweller. He needs 1 kg of gold every month to make gold and silver ornaments. Now he feels that if the demand for gold is high in 2-3 months, then the price of gold can increase. So, he buys a lot of 1 kg in gold futures. This is normal for him. If he has to buy gold anyway, then by buying an advance lot in futures, he can get protection against a possible price rise in this gold.

Similarly, if an oil company imports and refines crude oil, it is protected against possible price increases by buying a surfeit of crude oil in the commodity futures. There is a gram trader. One thousand sacks of gram are lying in his godown. He has to sell that gram anyway. If he sells the call at 5-10 percent above the spot price, then in future if the prices really rise, he has gram and he will get the higher price by delivery. If the price does not increase and his call expires without exercising, then he will get the premium without doing anything. This is a type of covered call about which you can learn more in my book How to Plant a Money Tree with Options Trading. You must have understood which category your competitors belong to. Now tell me which of the categories listed below do you belong:

1. Are you a big jeweller, who needs 1 kg or half kg of gold and silver per month?
2. Do you have a gram flour factory, in which 500-1000 bags of gram need to be bought per month for making gram flour?
3. Do you have a refinery which processes 100-200 barrels of crude oil per month?

If you don't fall into any the three categories then you are going to do commodity trading, which falls under futures and options, like speculation. You may be disappointed by my words. But you should understand the difference between speculation and investment. You don't have to be completely discouraged because, in this book, I will teach you to invest in commodity gold and silver in cash without going into future options. First let us understand through which exchanges the investment in the commodity market takes place.

There are three major commodity trading exchanges in India:

1. NCDEX or National Commodity and Derivatives Exchange
2. NMCE or National Multi Commodity Exchange of India Limited
3. MCX or Multi Commodity Exchange of India Limited

Commodity trading is done online on these exchanges in India, which is completely based on futures and options.

Selecting Broker for Commodity Trading: Brokers such as Zerodha, Upstox Angel Broking, IIFL, etc. offer online commodity trading facility in India. Commodity trading is regulated by the Forward Markets Commission. Commodity trading can be done in four categories:

1. **Metals:** Like-gold, silver, nickel, zinc, base metals etc.
2. **Energy:** Like-crude oil, coal, natural gas
3. **Livestock:** Animal-based production, such as wool, dairy products
4. **Agriculture:** Agriculture-based production, such as wheat, guar, gram, cotton, etc.

Mutual Funds or ETFs for Commodity Trading: Those who do not want to take the risk of Futures and Options for Commodity trading can invest in it through Mutual Funds or Index Funds and ETFs. Currently, ETFs are available in India for trading in gold and silver only.

Diversifying Portfolio by Commodity Trading:

This book will show you my own tried-and-tested way to diversify your portfolio and invest in commodities through ETFs in cash instead of trading commodities through futures and options. It is very important to have this diversity in the portfolio. I saw its direct benefit when the Russia-Ukraine war began in early 2022.

At that time the price of shares started falling badly. But those who had gold-silver ETFs were getting good returns as gold and silver prices rose during the war. The same was seen at the time of Corona - when the stock market fell, the price of gold was at an all-time high.

Therefore, instead of investing with cash in the portfolio, by investing in gold and silver according to my method, returns can also be earned on the cash which remains unutilized.

Currently, only gold and silver ETFs are available. In the future, if ETFs of other commodities also enter the market, then you can use this method in them, too. I have named this method 'Flow Method' because it allows you to have cash flow even when the market falls.

There is also another reason for naming it the 'flow method'. In this, the lowest level formed in the last five days is used. Therefore, the word Flow has been formed by joining F of FIVE in the English spelling of five and Low. I personally use this method for cash management. Although nothing can be safe in the stock and commodity market it can be considered the most secure method. The market risk will always be there anyway.

First of all, you have to decide how much you want to invest in a year through this method. I want to keep liquid cash of ₹ 2 lakhs to invest during a falling market so that when the market falls and if I need up to ₹ 2 lakhs to buy new shares, I can meet it with this ETF. You can decide as per your suitability how much you want to invest in a year through this method. Now I want to invest ₹ 2 lakhs in two ETFs, so the potential investment per ETF is 1 lakhs. Now I divide 1 lakhs into 52 weeks (there are about 52 weeks in 1 year). So, there will be an investment of about ₹ 1,923 per week in the share. Now in the flow method that I am going to explain, you have to place 5 GTT or VTC orders in 1 trading week. GTT order means Good till Trigger order and VTC order means Valid till Cancel order. Both the orders are valid for about

1 year once they are placed. But we need the order to be valid only for 5 days. For orders that are not triggered after 5 days, we will replace them with new orders. In this, you have to leave your GTT order for the next week on Saturday-Sunday which is the holiday of the market week. For that, the minimum level of that ETF has to be taken for the last 5 days of the market. For example, Saturday and Sunday were market holidays on the 26th and 27th respectively. In this, if you have to place an order to buy GoldBees (the highest volume traded gold ETF) for the next trading week, then look at the GoldBees price of the last trading week-

Date	Highest level	Lowest level	Close price
March 21, 2022	45.48	43.77	44.15
March 22, 2022	44.96	44.16	44.30
March 23, 2022	44.87	43.72	44.44
March 24, 2022	45.27	44.38	44.59
March 25, 2022	45.61	44.00	44.84

Now you have to place the GTT order for next week's buy by reducing 1 paisa each out of the 5 lows that were made in the last 5 days (previous trading week) on March 26-27, 2022. How many shares (ETF units) should we buy in each order? We have to invest 1,923 per week. When you place 5 orders like this in the last 5 days' low by reducing 1 paisa each, then next week you may not trigger a single order (if the gold price goes up), sometimes only 1 out of 5 orders will trigger, sometimes it may be 2-3 orders and sometimes there will be a fall in the price of gold and then all five of your orders will be triggered in that week.

My experience is that on average you will have 2 orders triggered in a week. Therefore, if you want to put an average of 1,923 per month, then it would be appropriate to put half of it, i.e. 961.50 in each order. That is, to the nearest integer, you have to place 5 orders of ₹ 1,000 each by reducing 1 paisa each in the last 5 days' low. That means while filling the order on March 26 and

27, 5 orders were to be placed, which are to be placed by placing buy orders of ₹ 1,000-1,000 at the prices of 43.76, 44.15, 43.71, 44.37, 43.99 respectively. Now in the next trading week, there were lows in the following way:

Date	Lowest level
March 28, 2022	44.27
March 29, 2022	43.88
March 30, 2022	43.88
March 31, 2022	43.99
April 1, 2022	43.15

Out of your 5 orders this week, all 5 orders would have been triggered by the price going down. Now we have to fill new orders again. There were only 4 orders at 44.20, 43.87, 43.98 and 43.14 which were down 1 paisa each from the last week's low because the same low of 43.88 was made on 2 days last week. So, we have to place only one order of 43.87 because there is no use in placing two orders at the same price.

In this system, you need considerable patience. You should not be greedy or avaricious at all because when these 5 orders will come, its price went up to 46.32 on April 19 due to the bull run of gold. Now your average price of about 44 will be shown as 46. You will feel that it is very interesting - you are getting 4-5 percent in about 18 days, so let's increase the capital in it. But you are wrong. Now if the price is falling, then even after your successive orders are triggered, you will also see a loss in holding. But this loss can show up to 5-10 percent of your buying average, not as much as in stocks. But don't panic and close at that time. Gradually, the average price will keep decreasing and when it bounces back, there will be a profit again.

Therefore, you do not have to increase the capital by being greedy nor reduce it by panicking. Now you will ask what will I do when there is a major fall in gold and silver prices and the price does not increase again for 15-20 years? If this happens, then the value of the jewellery lying in your home will also be less. Then you can sell these ETFs and buy jewellery made in return, which your wife will wear and you will pass on gold and silver to your generations as an inheritance.

Also, remember that if this happens then the other people using other methods will make more losses than you because you are buying little by little at less than the daily low levels. Therefore, your average price will always be low and if everything goes well and you invest around ₹ 1 lakh in 52 weeks, then you will see that your investment will often be 5-10-15 percent in profit and if there is a need for cash when there is a fall in the stock market, you will be able to buy shares in the fall by booking profit in it.

There is a very simple method for the readers who want to trade in it. Whenever you get more than 8 percent return from the average price, then book the profit and keep the system running. Overall, I consider this method to be the safest and consistently profitable in the commodity. The rest is speculation and in speculation, in the pursuit of more profit, the losses are also more.

To make gold and silver ornaments, a lot of hard work has to be done slowly with a small hammer; only then the attractive ornaments are made which are used on auspicious occasions for generations. To make an iron sword, it is stricken a few times with a thick hammer and then a sharp sword is made. You have to decide whether you want to walk on the edge of the sword by investing a large amount (big hammer) in futures and options or walk slowly with my method.

You can gradually invest the remaining ₹ 1 lakh in silver ETFs by using the above method. Here another question will arise. To understand that, see the data of silver ETF and GoldBees for the following 5 dates. NETF SILVER prices for the trading week of April 18 to April 22, 2022 were as follows:

Date	Highest level	Lowest leval	Close price
April 18, 2022	69.99	68.31	69.61
April 19, 2022	69.98	69.31	69.88
April 20, 2022	69.18	67.86	68.00
April 21, 2022	68.20	67.35	67.40
April 22, 2022	67.83	66.15	66.30

Now the market is closed on April 23-24, 2022 as it is Saturday-Sunday holiday and we have to place buy orders for ETF SILVER for the next trading week. As a rule, we should place 1,000 buy orders each at the lowest levels of the last five trading days i.e. 68.31, 69.31, 67.86, 67.35 and 66.15. But here the closing price of ETF SILVER on April 22, 2022 is 66.30, which is less than all four of them - 68.31, 69.31, 67.86 and 67.35.

When the closing price at the time of placing the order is 66.30, then there is no logic for placing a buy order at a price above that. So, in this case, only one order has to be placed at 66.15 as 66.15 is the only low of last week, which is less than the close of 66.30 at the end of the week.

Now you will ask, should you place the order of ₹ 1000 at 66.15 only or put the amount of the remaining orders in this and place an order of 5000? The answer is that you have to place an order for only one stake, i.e. 1000 at 66.15 because this type of position indicates that the silver market is in the bearish phase and prices may fall further. So, in such a situation, we have to place only one order on 66.15 for ₹ 1,000 only and the balance amount will be useful in the coming weeks. Similarly, from April 18, 2022 to April 22, 2022, the prices of GoldBees were also as follows:

Date	Highest Level	Lowest Level	Close Price
April 18, 2022	46.29	45.80	45.73
April 19, 2022	46.32	45+.63	46.19
April 20, 2022	47.49	44.93	45.98
April 21, 2022	47.60	45.09	45.22
April 22, 2022	45.84	45.08	45.21

In this too, the two-day lows of 45.80 and 45.63 are higher than the last close price of 45.21 and only three levels 44.93, 45.09, 45.08 are eligible to buy. In this also you will see that 45.09 and 45.08 are very close levels, with a difference of only ₹ 0.01.

So, if there is a difference of less than ₹ 0.10 between the two lowest levels, then they also have to be ignored and next week only two GTT orders have to be filled by reducing 44.93 by one paisa to 44.92 and 45.09 by 1 paisa to 45.08.

Therefore, at present, due to the availability of ETFs for only two commodities, i.e., gold and silver, one can gradually collect units in them by the method suggested. You can book profit whenever you get more than 8 percent profit from the average price, or you can keep them in place of cash in your account and buy shares by selling shares when the market falls.

You can also trade commodities directly on MCX through your Demat account. But in this method, you will be able to trade only in the futures options. Let's look at some of the major advantages and disadvantages.

Commodity trading offers many advantages as compared to other business segments. Most business investments provide investors with benefits in times of economic uncertainties. Some of the benefits are as follows:

Diversification of Portfolio

Commodity trading helps the trader to diversify his/her portfolio. By investing in commodities along with stocks, bonds and other avenues, the trader is able to hedge his losses from a sudden drop in one of his asset classes.

In addition, commodity trading responds differently to economic and geopolitical factors than stocks. Hence investing in commodities helps to improve returns and reduce volatility.

Hedging

Commodity acts as an effective hedge against risk, especially in times of inflation or recession. If the price of the commodity is expected to rise, the trader can buy the contract commodity and opt for hedging against the risk of higher prices. It is useful for importers and exporters.

Protection Against Inflation

When the economy declines, inflation rises and commodity prices rise. Stock and bond prices decline of fall during this time. But investing in commodities helps investors to benefit from the boom and protect them from high commodity prices.

Low Margin

The margin amount required for commodity trading is around 5-10 percent of the contract value, which is much lower compared to other asset classes. So, the trader can trade more with less money.

Higher Opportunities for Growth and Return

Commodity trading is very risky. But if the risk is well managed and the investment is done satisfactorily after proper research and analysis, then it can be very profitable. On account of the rapidly increasing demand for the commodity, commodity traders can grow and earn good money.

Liquidity

Investing in commodities is highly liquid compared to investing in other asset classes such as real estate, and buying and selling are much easier and faster. Hence the position can be easily squared off and encashed as and when required.

Commodity Trading Risks

Commodity trading, like all other forms of investing and trading, has many risks.

Risk increases when an investor enters the market unprepared or with very high expectations. Investors should be careful and trade according to their risk appetite. Some of the risks are as follows:

High Leverage

The margin amount required for commodity trading is quite low. So, there is high profit. However, high leverage can also act as a trap if not handled well. The businessman has a high chance of losing that money and thus can be burdened with enormous debt.

High Volatility

Commodities are quite risky in terms of volatility. The volatility in commodities is almost twice that in stocks and about four times that in bonds. Therefore, trading in the commodity market can be very risky for an inexperienced trader.

Lack of Experience

The basis of any form of business is experience and knowledge. Many new entrepreneurs don't educate themselves and jump into the business. Traders should read good commodity trading books, interact and share experiences with other experienced traders and prepare their own trading plans and strategies before beginning to practise trading. Thus, commodity trading is an interesting and rewarding process, which helps investors in hedging, speculation, and diversification of their portfolios. Also, the market is quite volatile and risky. Hence the trader should be careful before entering the market and should be focused, dedicated and diligent to make excellent profits and minimize losses.

- Investors can earn more profit in commodity trading as compared to other businesses.
- In addition, investors in commodity trading can diversify their portfolios.
- Commodity trading is risky. But if trading is done with the right strategy, the chances of return are also high.

My opinion on this is that if you are a small investor, then at present learn to earn safely in commodities like gold and silver by using the flow method. After that, other commodity ETFs will also surface, wherein you can earn safely through the flow method.

❑

16
Earning from Intraday Trading

"Never invest in a business you don't understand."

–Warren Buffett

Intraday trading means buying and selling securities (shares, commodities and currencies) etc. during the trading period of the stock exchange. In this, securities are bought and sold on the same day. That means, in intraday, securities are not bought with the intention of investing; in this, profits are made on account of price fluctuations throughout the day, too.

Difference Between Intraday and Delivery Trading: There are two ways of working in the stock market- (1) intraday trading, and (2) delivery trading.

1. **Intraday Trading:** In this, trading is done on margin. Hence it requires less capital. For example, if your broker operates on a margin of 10 percent, you can buy 1 lakh shares by paying a 10,000 margin. Due to this, if the share increases by 1 percent, then you will have a profit of 1,000, which is a profit of 10 percent of your invested capital. This is called leverage. As you were told at the beginning of the book, this same leverage can prove to be fatal for you.

For example, if you had not placed a stop-loss in the said trade and the stock had fallen by 10 percent for some reason, then you would have lost 10,000 i.e. your entire capital would have been wiped out. Therefore, intraday trading has the following positive and negative aspects:

Positive Aspects

1. Large positions can be taken on margin in intraday with less capital.
2. It involves less brokerage as compared to delivery.
3. In this, profit can be made fast.
4. Short selling can be done in this, that is, you can sell the shares without holding them and buy them back before the market closes. This is called short selling, which involves selling first and then buying. Profits can be made by short selling even in a falling market.

Negative Aspects

1. In intraday, it is decided that you have to cut your position before the market closes. That's why, for a short period of time, when big traders see your position on screen and know what your time horizon is, they can create an artificial bullish trend/recession by placing large orders in the stock and wipe your capital by simply triggering your stop-loss. Those who are traders must have realized that whenever they put a stop-loss, only then their stock triggers the stop-loss and turns back. This is described in more detail in my book 41 Trading Tips.
2. Intraday trading offers high returns, but at the same time, the risk is high. Intraday trading carries the highest risk and is absolutely unsafe for novice traders. Remember - intraday trading is more difficult than it seems. If you want to get an idea of its risk, then when you meet a person who says that the stock market is very dangerous, stay away from the stock

market and that he lost all the capital in the stock market, you should ask him, "Did you do intraday in the stock market or did you do delivery-based business? For how long did you stay in the stock market?" The answer would be 100 percent that he used to deal in intraday or futures options. He must have been ruined before completing 3 years in the stock market and bade goodbye. Here I mean to say that even in delivery, you have to invest your capital gradually by dividing it into 33 to 40 parts. It is also necessary to be patient. An understanding of the market develops after spending 3 years. To secure intraday trading, traders must have considerable expertise, experience and reasoning, which comes after years of practice and dedication. That's why I have written that the trader who has been ruined must have been ruined before 3 years.

Delivery Business: In this, shares are bought by paying cash, which are stored in your Demat account. In this, you have bought a part of the business by buying shares which are now your property. Now it is your choice whether you sell it after 1 day or sell it after 1 year or sell it after 10 years. So, in this, it is not easy for big traders to tap you. But in this also, you should not invest big capital at once. To win in the stock market, it is very important for you to have cash management. To buy new shares, you should have a steady cash flow or you should avoid investing too much by being greedy or over confident. Divide the capital into 33-40 parts and invest each part gradually and before the capital runs out, that is, when 20-25 parts are invested, then you should be cautious and maintain cash even by booking small profits so that you don't run out of cash when the market falls heavily.

Now let's talk about how to earn money in intraday trading. Because there are traders with more than 3 years' experience and they want to do intraday only, it is also my duty to tell them about the method in this book. You will find many tools for intraday trading, such as Momentak, Moving Average Crossover Breakout, etc. Seeing chart analysis and technical indicators from around the world, you will be lost as to which strategy to use, which indicators to use and which not to use.

In this book, I will explain to you a smart strategy because according to me only that strategy is the easiest and most successful. Some key points have to be followed in this:

1. Select the stock for intraday only from the top 500 stocks with the highest market cap.

2. Don't take positions on only one side, i.e., no matter what the market looks like, you must strike a balance between buy (long side) and sell (short side) positions. I will explain further how this balance should be achieved.

3. Do not take a position of more than ₹ 10,000 (Ten thousand) in a share. This 10,000 is not the margin but it is the total position value. That means if your broker gets the intraday done at a 20 percent margin, then put a maximum margin of ₹ 2,000 in a share and do not take a position more than ₹ 10,000 in total. This will have two advantages—one is that your intraday portfolio will be diversified i.e., there will be many different positions and secondly, due to small positions, big traders will not want to waste their time tapping you and they will find greedy prey with a big position.

4. In the super breakout method described in the chapter on Technical Analysis, I have told you that you can identify the above stocks to buy and sort with the help of Google Sheets. You will find this google sheet on my blog and you can also search and watch a video of mine which highlights how to do intraday from super breakout.

   Overall, the stocks that are above the 5, 10, 15, and 100-day average and below the 200-day average have to be selected to buy. Conversely, those that fall below the 5, 10, 15, 50 and 100 days average and are above the 200-day average have to be chosen to sell. Make a diary of such shares and keep writing in it because they do not have to be bought and sold immediately.

I have in my video the above method that when the selected shares from Super Breakout goes over 200 DMA they have to be bought and when the selected stock goes below 200 DMA they have to be sold. Confused?

Never mind, I will give an example. Hindalco's stock was at 493 and had come down from its 5, 10, 15, 50, 100 DMA. Its 200 DMA was ₹ 487.30. Now you filled the sell order at the trigger of 487.30 and it got triggered, but it went back to 476.45 and came back to 491. This is called taking support at 200 DMA. But you could have got it easily by keeping a 1 percent profit target in this method. In this way, in this super breakout sheet, fill the order with the stop loss trigger price in all the shares that fall in the buy-sell range and once the stock is triggered, then place the stop loss.

5. The most standard profit target should be between 0.80 to 1.20 percent as per your convenience. Keep the stop loss in the range of 0.40 to 0.60 percent of the trigger price, i.e., keep the stop loss at half the target.

6. One particular point - those who calculate 200 DMA in Google Sheet and match the 200 DMA given on Money Control and place an order only with the correct 200 DMA given on them.

According to the above, while trading in intraday you should also remember that neither will you profit in all positions, nor will you gain profit every day. In this, you have to take the overall profit. For example, in a day, 3 shares were triggered on the buy side and 2 shares on the sell side and you put a stop loss at 0.50 percent and a target of 1 percent, then the stop loss will be triggered in some and the target will be triggered in some. Overall, if you are in profit, then you can earn income in a month by making small profits. If you take large positions in intraday, then the risk is high whereas, in small positions, the income is less. Therefore, in the next chapter, the method of margin trading will be highlighted, which is better than intraday. If you have an account with SBI Securities, you can convert the intraday position to e-margin at the end of the day. This will give you 30 days extra time and SBI Securities does not charge interest on it for 30 days.

Some Points to be Particularly Kept in Mind for Intraday

Various strategies are used by intraday traders. But using the right strategy at the right time is the key. Actually, trading is an art, which gradually develops with practice. I will tell you what things you should keep in mind to develop this art.

Business with Current Trends

When the market is bullish, the intraday trader should choose those stocks which are likely to rise. When the market is bearish, they should look for stocks that may decline. Intraday trends change rapidly. These changes should be observed carefully and that pattern should be caught and then followed.

Putting Emotions Aside

An intraday trader should keep his emotions aside and not get overly influenced by profit or loss. In fact, losses should be taken into account and learned from. An intraday trader should be patient and wait for the pullback so that he can enter and exit with less risk.

Make a Business Plan

Start with deciding whether you want to trade in intraday or delivery business! Then, make a detailed plan for intraday trading.

Strategies should be studied and then the most suitable one should be chosen. Before the start of each trading day, a plan should be made and profit and loss should be tracked to know which strategy is most effective. In my opinion, it is more effective to buy swing trades in cash rather than intraday because you will never be able to take more positions by using full cash rather than using margin.

Avoid Over-Trading

A disciplined intraday trader should be slow. When there is no clear trend in the market, then trading should not be done till the market is stable. Make sure the range of movement of prices is high enough so that profits outweigh the potential risks. Do not trade when the market is not rising or falling.

Market Order and Limit Order Status

In a limit order, the maximum buy price is determined by an order and similarly, in a sell order, the minimum sell price is determined by an order. If the market does not reach the limit order, the order will not be executed. It is therefore advisable to set a limit order instead of a market order to ensure that there are no unpleasant losses.

Keep Learning

It is essential to do intraday trading as a full-time business where the learning never ends. A skilled intraday trader should have an open mind to learn rather than being stubborn and rigid.

Use Stop Loss

Stop loss helps to prevent losses at a particular point and covers the position if the price moves beyond a specific range. Thus, it keeps the trader away from emotions and keeps capital safe. Therefore, massive losses can be avoided by using stop loss. I personally do not support stop loss. But not placing stop loss is only for those who, according to me, do only delivery-based cash trading in Nifty 50 or Top 10 blue-chip or ETFs or REIT, INVITs, etc. If you do intraday, then placing a stop loss also becomes necessary.

Intraday trading requires a very different set of qualities, abilities and mental setup. It is not necessary that everyone is successful in intraday trading. Statistically, only 4 to 5 percent of intraday traders are able to earn for a long time. However, if one wants to try and be good at intraday trading, then it requires one to be dedicated, diligent, consistent, and very open to learning.

One must understand all the positive and negative aspects and know that they have the desire and ability to be an intraday trader as intraday trading involves long working hours, emotional trauma, high-risk appetite, and constant learning. Get into intraday trading only once you are prepared for it. Otherwise, if you want to take advantage of leverage, switch to margin trading instead of intraday, which will be described in the next chapter.

❑

17
Earning from Margin Trading

"Many people invest themselves only when other people are investing. But the right time to make more profit is when one is not investing."

–Warren Buffett

Margin trading is the process by which a trader can borrow money from brokers and use that money to buy securities. I had read a book by a famous author, in which the author insists only on investing in real estate. The author's argument for this is that in real estate, you get the benefit of leverage and any bank will give you a loan to buy property easily; but if you go and ask for a loan to buy shares, the bank manager will laugh at you and throw you out of the bank.

The words of this writer may have been correct in those times. But today, most of the brokers for margin trading provide loans, i.e. margin. Basically, margin trading is a method of buying more shares by paying less amount in the cash market. This way, you are allowed to buy shares worth 100 percent amount by your broker by giving 25 percent to 40 percent margin. For example, 30 percent margin is payable on NiftyBees, where you can buy NiftyBees for 1 lakh by paying 30,000. Your broker will lend you the balance amount of ₹ 70,000 (seventy thousand rupees) and in return, you will have to pledge your shares with your stockbroker.

Most brokers also charge interest on this lent amount, which can range from 12 percent to 10 percent annually, and the interest is charged on a daily basis. In this book, I am going to tell you the method of taking margin at 0 (zero) percent interest rate. But before that, understand the risk in margin trading. Don't panic after reading about the risk. Next, I will also tell you the method of managing this risk.

In fact, when you buy shares of a greater amount by paying less amount of income on margin, though you get more profit from it the chances of loss are also high. For example, if you took a position of 10,000 by paying a margin of 3,300 and your stock falls by 20 percent instead of increasing, then your loss on 3,300 is ₹ 2,000, which is a loss of more than half of your invested capital.

There is another risk - the margin is calculated by the exchange on the basis of the daily price of the share. If your stock falls by 15-20 percent, then an additional margin will be demanded by the exchange. If you are unable to pay the additional margin, your position will be squared off, i.e., your shares will be sold at a loss.

So, margin trading needs to be done with a care and prudence. Most brokers offer the facility to buy shares on margin for 365 days. For example, if you buy Infosys shares of ₹ 25,000 with a margin of ₹ 6,000, the remaining 19,000 is lent to you by your broker and he charges an interest of 12 percent per annum. Different brokers charge interest at different rates. So, this interest will be charged on a daily basis, which will be around ₹ 6.25 per day.

If you book profit after 10 days, then on the basis of ₹ 6.25 per day, you will have to pay interest of ₹ 62.50 for 10 days. If you keep this position on credit for the entire 365 days, then about ₹ 2,281.25 will be spent on interest alone. Therefore, do not hold the margin position for more than 30 days. After that, if you want, you can take its delivery so that there is no burden of much interest. After giving the above initial information about margin trading, I will explain my method to you that how we can earn more profit without paying interest in margin trading.

Suppose you have ₹ 5 lakhs. Now there are two methods of making this margin investment – one method is used by the common unaware investor. He directly makes a guess and creates a position of ₹ 1.50 lakhs by giving a margin of 50,000 in any higher running blue-chip. If there is a 5 percent profit on this, then he is happy that he has earned ₹ 7,500. Now he greedily invests the entire ₹ 5 lakhs on margin in 5-10 shares. After that he starts earning - sometimes 7,500, sometimes 15,000, sometimees 22,500 every day. He elated.

But the market never grows continuously. One day the market starts falling for one reason or the other. He thinks that it doesn't matter, it will rise again. But when the market is in recession, it does not go up so quickly. Now his entire 5 lakhs gets stuck and all his shares incur a 10 to 15 percent loss. Additionally, ₹ 165 starts getting deducted as interest from his account every day. When the stock falls, the exchange also asks for an additional margin of around ₹ 50,000, which he does not have. Finally, his broker sells his position at a loss of 25-30 percent and books the loss.

Now he has incurred a loss of about ₹ 1.50 lakhs. He also has to pay about 20-30 thousand in interest, share pledge charges, brokerage, GST etc. He regrets that he has hardly earned 50-60 thousand and lost 1.80 lakhs. This is the method of the unaware trader, which most new investors try. They then curse the market after losing ₹ 1.5-2 lakhs. If they have seen a video about the margin by a research analyst like me skipping some parts, then they abuse him in the comments section. Now let's talk about the share genius method of investing in the margin.

In this, first of all, a margin account has to be opened in SBI Securities. (I am not an agent of SBI. But at present, the interest rate on margin in SBI is zero percent. That's why I am talking about opening a margin account in it.) You can also find the link to open an account in SBI Securities on my blog www.maheshkaushik.com. SBI Securities provides an e-margin facility.

In this, no interest is charged for 30 days, i.e., in e-margin for 30 days we can carry our position without interest.

Now in the method of Share Genius Margin Trading, only one company's shares have to be bought on margin every day; that too if the total capital is ₹ 5 lakhs, then do not buy more than worth 15,000. If your total capital is 10 lakhs, then you have to buy 30,000 shares of a company daily and if the total capital is ₹ 2.50 lakhs, then that amount will be 7,500. You have to first decide the maximum amount to be invested in a company according to the total capital.

Now which company shares will you buy? The google sheet of the technical analysis super breakout method described in this book will be found on my blog. Those who are on the top side of buying shares will buy shares of 15,000 on margin, that is, by giving a margin of about 5,000, they have to buy 15,000 shares, i.e., 5,000 cash and 10,000 loan - a total of 15,000 shares.

Now the google sheet of the super breakout method shows that the following stocks have gone over their 5, 10, 15, 50 and 100 DMA and below 200 DMA and according to the technical analysis, they have to be bought at the trigger point of 200 DMA.

PETRONET

MRF

GICARE

LICHSGFIN

Now if you had taken it in intraday, you would have taken it on the trigger point of 200 DMA. But in margin trading, we are going to hold for 30 days anyway and these stocks are now on the verge of the super breakout. So, you have to buy the topmost PETRONET share on margin at market price without waiting for the breakout.

Here we are talking about the automatic google sheet of the super breakout method available on my blog. This sheet includes the companies with the 500 highest market caps and is arranged in descending order of market cap. Therefore, the stock that appears at the top will be the one with the highest market cap among these stocks. If you have a total of 5 lakhs, then you have to buy a total of 15,000 shares by putting a margin of about 5,000 in it. Now the next day when you saw the sheet, its situation was as follows.

1. HUL
2. PETRONET
3. ROUTE
4. BBTC

So, now with HUL at the top, you will buy shares worth 15,000 in that too by putting a margin of about 5,000. On the third day when you look at the sheet again, suppose it looks like this.

1. HUL
2. BRITANNIA
3. PERONET
4. PFC
5. NHPC

So, now you already have HUL on hold. That's why you have to choose BRITANNIA at number 2. In this way, we will view the sheet from top to bottom. Leaving the stock which is already held, we will continue to choose whatever new share comes first from top to bottom. Now when it is 29 days for the first stock (we will get 30 days free margin), then we will see if there is more than 5 percent profit and then we will sell them. Otherwise, we will take delivery of the remaining margin after paying 10,000. We have to do this in all stocks. After 29 days, if the shares earn more than 5 percent profit, then we will book the profit, or else we will take delivery.

Whenever there is more than 5 percent profit in the shares which have been taken for delivery, we will also sell them. If a stock taken in a delivery gives a sell signal from the super breakout sheet, i.e. it comes below 5, 10, 15, 50, 100 DMA, then only what is above 200 DMA, we will take 200 DMA as stop loss and whenever it goes below 200 DMA, you can book a loss by selling it as that money will come back to you. When the stock shows a sign of going up again, then it can be bought at a lower price than the price at which it was sold. This is called reverse trading.

Now let's talk about money management. Let's say none of your shares are sold (in the worst situation) for the whole month. You will invest ₹ 1 lakh in 20 stocks in 20 days at the rate of 5,000. You still have ₹ 4 lakh cash with you. Now if the recession continues for the next month also, then you will have to take delivery of 20 shares for the first month by paying 10,000 per share. So, about 2 lakhs get invested in taking delivery and if you buy 20 new shares next month also, then 1 lakh margin will go in them. That is, if no shares are sold even for 2 months, then to run this system, about 4 lakhs of cash will be needed and you have ₹ 5 lakhs. That is, no matter how deplorable the situation is, you will have the cash to run the system for about two and a half to three months and there will be no interest due to the free margin for 30 days in SBI.

However, the situation of continuous decline for two and a half months will not come in it. Most of your shares will earn more than 5 percent and will continue to rotate. However, to successfully earn in the stock market, cash should not be low during the recession. Therefore, a condition of 15,000 has been placed on 5 lakhs. It is also in line with the rule that you divide your total capital into 33-40 parts and then invest 1 part each in different shares. You can invest the remaining unused cash in gold and silver by the flow method as described in the chapter on commodities and you can withdraw cash by selling gold and silver ETFs as needed.

Another important point was mentioned in the chapter on Intraday that margin is a better method than trading. I had not just wade an off the cuff comment. In SBI, you can also convert intraday positions to e-margin. For example, if you do intraday and if your intraday position is not in profit then you can change it to e-margin. This will give you 30 days.

I hope you have understood this method and using it you will be able to earn regular profits by trading more intelligently in the margin.

❑

18
Earning from Algo Trading

"Stock market is the act of moving from active (quickly trading more than stop loss) to tolerant (buying at the right time and holding patiently)."

–Warren Buffett

Algo trading is an advanced method. In this, a set of instructions is given to the computer in the form of an algorithm to receive signals to buy and sell a stock. Based on the algorithm of these instructions, the computer analyses and gives buy and sell signals for the shares. The process of placing orders based on these signals is called Algo trading.

Algo trading is a very effective method. In this, you don't need to look at your screen continuously to find business opportunities. When a trade signal is received, the algorithm automatically detects and gives you a buy/sell signal. This saves the business from possible mistakes.

At present, about 40 percent of trading on NSE is done through Algo trading. Large institutional investors, high net worth investors and some retail investors are beginning to benefit from algo trading. But Algo trading in India is legally recognized only for institutional investors. SEBI allowed Algo trading for institutional investors in 2008 and orders of retail investors still cannot be filled completely automatically through algorithms. Yet retail investors can easily be confused by the name of Algo trading and trading software.

Now you will say that some brokerage companies allow you to create algos and trade based on it. In fact, as there is no legal recognition, such companies send SMS to you when the buy-sell signal of shares comes on the basis of your algo. You have to take the decision of executing the final trade.

Beware of Fake Companies and Fake Software: There are many ending software being sold in the market. Actually, it is human nature that a fraudulent person wants to earn money without working hard. Even in the stock market, he keeps looking for automatic methods that can earn him money with work.

I have a friend. He told me that though there is profit in your methods like Darvas Box Method, Share Genius Saving Trading, Turtle Trading etc, there is a lot of hard work involved, and there are too many problems in applying and updating GTT every day.

I explained to him that it hardly takes half an hour to feed and update orders daily. Can't you work even half an hour to earn money? Look at a shopkeeper. He earns his living by working hard for 12-14 hours from morning till night. Then a friend of mine said that my example is not practical. The shopkeeper is different, the stock market is different. Tell me a method, whereby once you invest, you keep earning continuously.

I stopped arguing with him. But later I noticed that he kept buying trading software from different companies and wasting money. Finally, he gave up and declared investing in stocks as rubbish and is currently mining cryptocurrencies.

So, always keep in mind that no method, no software, no algo can make 100 percent money for you without hard work. For this, you have to put your mind to work, too. A method that worked today will not work tomorrow. Therefore, you cannot earn from the stock market by relying on any one algorithm or one software. That's why I am always in favour of dividing the capital into several parts and investing a small amount using all methods. Do not invest it all at once, always ensure that you have enough cash left to invest at every level of the market.

I will give one more example. I met a security guard. He was very happy to see me. He asked me if I guide people on the stock market on YouTube. When I said yes, he told me very eagerly and enthusiastically that he also deals in options trading in the stock market and earns 10 to 15 thousand daily. Now I was shocked as to which options trading gave him 10 to 15 thousand daily. Then he told me that he was doing algo trading. I told him that algo trading was not legal for retail investors and asked him how he was doing it.

Then the security personnel told me that he has taken a company's subscription plan, wherein the company took the ID and password of his trading account after he paid the annual subscription charge (about ₹ 50 thousand). Now by putting indiscriminate trade call-puts from his account, it was showing him to be in daily profit.

I explained to him that all this would be profitable only for a few days during the trial period. Then his stop loss will be triggered. He didn't believe me. He looked at me and said, "How would that happen? The company has software and keeps small stop losses. It can never happen that all my capital will be wiped away."

After a few days, the security personnel met me again. So, I asked him how his algo trade was going. Then he observed that options trading was a gamble and the stock market was rubbish and that one should never attempt it. It is better to do a job and enjoy oneself. On prodding further, he said that sometime after the trial period, his stop loss got triggered. Every day at the end of the day, a loss of 15-20 thousand started appearing. Frightened by this, he called the company and was told that it was common to see this happen. In Algo trading, they keep small stop losses. But by taking more trades and adding small losses, it became 15-20 thousand. In a few days, if the movement of the market becomes stable, then all these losses will be recovered. Then the Russia-Ukraine war began and his trading account showed a loss of ₹ 1.25 lakhs in a single day. The company said that their stop loss was not triggered due to the sharp drop.

In this way, after a gradual loss of ₹ 3-5 lakhs, when he panicked and changed the password of the trading account, the company stopped answering his calls. Overall, you should avoid falling into the trap of such bogus algo companies and software vendors. You should develop your own algorithm by putting the formula on Google Finance Sheet. Based on that, you should trade from small portions of the capital at your discretion.

My YouTube channel has many ways to trade from your own algorithms from Google Finance Sheets. The following are the three main methods:

1. **Share Genius Method with Bottom Out Hunting Filter:** In this, first those stocks are scanned in the Google Finance Sheet which have recently made an annual low (52-week low). This is called bottom-out hunting or BOH filter. After this, by putting the formula of 20-day low level in it, those stocks are marked, which have reached their 20-day low level. Now let's start filling GTT orders at the 20-day high of these stocks. Gradually over time, if the 20-day high level comes down then keep reducing it. Whenever such a stock rises again, a buy signal is triggered.

   I use this method myself. It is briefly described in the book. If you search by typing Sharegenius Saving Trading With BOH Filter on YouTube and watch its video, then you will understand completely. You can also download the sheet with its formula from my blog and use these formulas to set the algo on Chartink.

2. **Turtle Trading with BOH Filter:** In this, a 55-day high is used instead of a 20-day high. This method also works very well. This is the method I use in my wife's trading account. For this, search by typing Turtle Trading With BOH Filter Mahesh Kaushik and download the relevant sheets and formulas and make a scanner on Google Sheets or Chartink.

3. **Super Breakout Method:** This is what I use for e-margin trades in my SBI account. It has been described in the technical analysis chapter 'Intraday Walker Chapter' and 'Margin Trading' chapter of this book.

Thus, my advice is to avoid buying software for algo trading or giving money to anyone. With some hard work, learn from YouTube and make your own scanner of google finance sheet or Chartink, which will keep giving signals to buy/sell based on algorithms.

Now I will tell you about the kind of algorithms that are used by big institutional investors. This is being told for informational purposes only. So, don't worry if you don't understand the details of the following algorithms.

Momentum and Trend-Based Strategy

This Algo Trading Strategy is the simplest and most widely used one.

It follows the trends and movements in the market and the business is executed accordingly. Technical indicators such as moving averages and price level movements are studied and based on these technical indicators, buy or sell orders are placed when a set of conditions are met.

The momentum and trend-based strategy also analyses the historical and current price data to see if the trend is likely to continue and makes decisions accordingly. Complex predictions are not prepared; just a simple and easy trend is followed. The business is executed if the desired event occurs; if it does not, it is not executed.

A common example is - the algorithm can be set up in such a way that the system is directed to buy the shares of a company when the 30-day moving average moves above the 180-day moving average and sell if the 30-day moving average moves below the 180-day moving average. This strategy is a simple definition of technical indicators.

Arbitrage Strategy

Arbitrage opportunities exist when there is a price difference between shares on different stock exchanges. Arbitrage strategy is one of the algo trading strategies, which uses these arbitrage opportunities to identify and exploit them as quickly as possible using computers.

If a stock is priced low on one exchange and high on another, the algorithm immediately detects the price difference, executes a trade to buy on the lower-priced exchange, and sell on the higher priced exchange.

This is where the speed and accuracy of algo trading play an important role as compared to human trading. Since the price difference between the exchanges is not very large, the volume needs to be kept high enough to be profitable in this type of trading. This strategy is mostly applicable in the case of forex trading.

As an example of strategy, Infosys is listed on both NSE and NYSE.

The algorithm receives feeds from both the exchanges regarding the company's stock price and will convert the price in one currency to another with the help of forex rates. If the algorithm finds a significant difference between the two listings due to currency rates, it will automatically place a buy order on the lower-priced exchange and a sell order on the higher-priced exchange. Once the order is executed, the trader gets the arbitrage profit.

Mean Reversal Strategy

Mean Reversal Strategy is one of the Algo trading strategies. It is based on the basic premise that the share prices can go higher or lower, but they come back to the mean price after some time. It is also known as a counter-trend or reversal strategy.

This strategy captures the upper and lower price ranges of the stock and the algorithm works to execute orders when it is beyond the normal range. The algorithm calculates the average price based on the stock's historical data and executes a trade hoping that the prices will return to the average price.

This means that if the prices are too high, they will go down and if they are too low, they will go up.

Hence this Algo trading strategy is useful when prices are at their peak and traders can profit from unexpected swings. However, this strategy can also backfire when prices do not actually rebound relatively fast.

For example, when the stock is below the 30-day moving average, the 90-day moving average, it is believed that the prices are too low and will approach the 90-day moving average. It signals the algorithm to buy the shares.

Statistical Arbitrage Strategy

Statistical arbitrage is one of the short-term Algo trading strategies. This trading is based on opportunities that arise due to price inefficiencies and misalignment of the price of shares. It occurs in shares which are related to each other or are similar in nature. It is now clear that inefficiency and wrong prices do not last very long.

They tend to settle in a short period of time and hence Algo trading becomes an effective way to capture them and make profits. In this case, the algorithm consists of complex mathematical models, which detect price inefficiencies early and execute trades before prices are back on track.

A human trader may not be able to track such changes, even if he is extremely dedicated, aware and up-to-date. But the algorithm, because of the pre-determined instructions, tracks them as they occur. As an example of strategy, both Bajaj Auto and Hero MotoCorp are somehow related to each other in terms of share pricing.

If the price of Bajaj falls, then the price of Hero should also go down. But due to market inefficiency, the price of one goes up. Based on the statistical arbitrage strategy, the algorithm will immediately detect the decline in the share price of Hero and buy it and then sell it later when the price is right resulting in a profit.

Weight Average Price Strategy

This is one of the most efficient Algo trading strategies. It is based on either the volume average price or the time average price. In this strategy the orders are large, but they are not shipped all at once. Orders are issued in small portions using a stock's historical volume profile or a certain number of defined time slots between start and end times.

The objective of this strategy is to execute orders as close to the volume average price or time average price as possible in order to minimize the impact on the market. Computers and algorithms play a vital role in issuing orders in small portions and do so with greater efficiency and precision that is not possible by humans.

The overall summary is that you should develop your own algo with the help of Google Finance Sheets or Chartink scanner so that you know when to buy and when to sell shares. For those who know a smattering of maths and do not have much technical knowledge, I have put such Google Sheets on my blog for free use and have also explained in the videos on YouTube about how to use them.

❑

19
Earning from Currency Trading

Currency trading is also called forex trading. Forex trading basically means buying and selling of currency. Forex trading is one of the largest financial markets in the world. More than 5 trillion are traded in forex daily. Forex trading takes place all over the world, so forex trading is done 24 hours a day in one or other country around the world.

Currency trading in India is regulated by RBI and SEBI as currency trade affects the economy of the country. If the rupee depreciates beyond a certain limit, the RBI intervenes and starts selling, which stops the fall in the rupee. Therefore, as there is not much volatility in currency trading, there is less possibility of very rapid profit and loss in it.

Currency trading is a better option for traders who do not want to take a risk in futures and options as there aren't sharp losses in it. Apart from investors and traders in the currency market, many big companies, central banks of different countries, travellers travelling from one country to another, etc. deal in it.

Companies also make deals to hedge their positions in the currency market. Currency trading in India is done through NSE.

Currency trading takes place in pairs, such as Dollar-INR, Dollar-Euro, Euro-Pound, Yen-INR etc. In India, you can trade forex in the following currency pairs:

1. USD INR
2. EURO INR
3. GBP INR
4. JYP INR
5. GBP USD
6. EUR USD
7. USD JPY

If you trade in USD/INR pairs, USD will be called the base currency and INR will be called the quotation currency. You can buy lots in USD/INR futures. The lot size in this is 1,000 dollars. Worldwide, the value of a currency is written down to the fourth point of the decimal. This is called PIP or Percentage in Points. The pip base for USD/INR is 0.0025, which means the minimum price difference will be 0.0025 and the price will convert to its coefficient. Currently, currency futures expire every Friday and deals with weekly expiry are available. But you can also do trades with a maturity of up to one year, e.g., in May 2022 USD/INR futures with the expiry of May 27, 2022, was trading at 77.5725, and at the same time the lot with the expiry of April 26, 2023, was also trading at the same time. It was trading at 80.0775 and had a volume of 15,314 lots by 1 am.

The major reason why trading in currency futures is popular is that it has high leverage and positions are available with only a 2.5 percent margin. For example, if you buy a 1,000-dollar lot at 77.57250 with an expiry of May 27, 2022, then the total value of your transaction would have been 77,572.50 paise and you would have got a position in 1 lot in it with a margin of only 2.5 percent i.e., ₹ 1,938.17. If its price had increased by only 0.20 points, i.e., 77.7725, then you would have earned ₹ 200 per 1000 lot, in which by reducing the brokerage of ₹ 40, ₹ 160 would have been saved.

Owing to the gradual change in the price of currency futures, the risk is less in them. But on the basis of this, it cannot be said that it is not at all risky. Sometimes there can be a big move in them too and you can suffer a major loss. But they carry the least risk as compared to derivatives deals in equities and commodities.

If you want to earn money from currency trading, then the best method is 'Calendar Spread Method'. In this, both buy and sell positions are created in different expiry months.

Calendar Spread Method: I will try to explain the Calendar Spread Methods to you with a very simple example. The rate of USD INR on NSE as on May 9, 2022 was 77.6075 at the price of May 27, 2022, and the future rate for the next month's expiry on June 28, 2022 was 77.8575.

It usually happens that long-distance futures have higher premiums and shorter-range futures have lower premiums. Now in this, you have to buy a lot with the expiry on May 27, 2022 and sell a lot with the expiry of June 28, 2022. This will hedge your position. That means, now if the price of the US dollar goes up/down, you will gain in one position and lose in the other. But if you have already bought and sold lots and made arbitrage with a difference of 0.25, then overall you will be more likely to make a profit.

While making arbitrage in this, keep in mind that you have to make an arbitrage only when there is a difference of 0.25 point or more in total. While making the arbitrage, do not consider LTP only, but make the deal only after seeing the actual ask price and bid price also because lest the price at which you place the order be different from the ask price and the bid price, the trade will be executed at a different price.

To understand the profit better in calendar spread, you should do paper trade, i.e., note the fictitious deals on paper and check daily what would have happened if you had taken the real deal. Once you have a thorough grasp of the paper trade, you can create real deals as well.

How to Get Daily Household Expense Amount from Currency Trading?

The headline about deriving the amount for daily household expenses from currency trading must have sounded very appealing. I keep getting many e-mails, in which followers want me to tell them some method by which they can earn ₹ 400-500 daily through intraday and keep their household expenses running. In fact, people in foreign countries also do this, and when we see such videos of foreign people such a desire awakens in our minds, as well.

If you want to do that, then the option of doing intraday in equities is riskier. Compared to this, making a calendar spread in currency is the least risky, and only about a 4,000 to 5,000 margin is required to make a calendar spread.

Since there is no guarantee of return in any trade, the method that I will describe here is neither guaranteed nor is it risk-free. But it has higher earning potential and less risk as compared to equity. So, use this method at your own discretion. Please do not hold me responsible if any damage is caused by your greed or careless use.

In this method, a calendar spread is created in all those currency pairs with a higher volume of currency in intraday, whose price difference is more than 0.25. That is, a lot of currency is bought in the future of this month's expiry and the lot of the expiry of the next month is sold for at least 0.25 more. It is fine if you get more difference than this, but it should not be less than that.

Not more than one lot is taken in any position and these positions are also held in intraday only. All the positions are exited together if all the positions have an aggregate profit of 200-400 after brokerage.

Overall, currency trading is the most comprehensive and most advanced form of trading. To earn in this, you need to develop an understanding of finding business opportunities. In this, options is also traded and like equity, the call-put of currency is also sold. You can also trade in options and buy lots of currency pairs in futures and sell covered calls in the option. This is called Poor Main Covered Call, where instead of holding the actual currency, you hold a lot of the future and sell the call at the higher level in the option.

Apart from the calendar spread, there are some other methods for trading in currency, which are as follows:

Price Action Strategy

This is one of the simplest and most commonly used forex trading strategies.

In this strategy, the previous price data of the currency is studied that after falling to which price the currency shows the back stimulus and after rising to which price it shows a decline. Based on these support and resistance levels, the fair price to buy and sell the currency is estimated.

The biggest strength of the price action strategy is that it works in all market conditions, whether it is trending or volatile or less volatile.

An example of a price action strategy is the Blade Runner strategy, which uses candlesticks, pivot points, round numbers, and support and resistance levels. The 20-day DMA is used in the Blade Runner strategy. A short position is taken when once the price goes below the 20-day DMA and back up, and then again if it goes below the 20-day DMA.

Trend Trading Strategy

Trend trading is one of the most successful forex trading strategies. As the name suggests this strategy involves identifying and following the trend. To identify the direction of the trend, traders can use tools such as moving averages, stochastics, relative strength indicators and others. Currency prices are also influenced by trends in global events such as inflation, interest rate policy, and government policy. Therefore, it is necessary for a trend-based trader to keep an eye on the news from around the world so that he can take advantage of it.

Breakout Trading Strategy

One of the effective currency trading strategies is the breakout trading strategy. Under this strategy, the trader goes to the market at a time when the market is outside its previous trading range.

If the price moves higher than the previous resistance level, the trader can expect the price to move higher by entering this breakout point. Similarly, if the price crosses the previous support level, the trader can sell at that point in anticipation of a further downside in the market.

There is a level of consolidation before the price moves up, where the prices remain in a stable range. Prices often hit support and resistance levels just before a breakout, when the trader wants to enter or exit the market. The breakout trading strategy becomes very attractive to the forex trader because the market is prone to high volatility and breakouts, both real and unreal. The forex trading market is known for high volume trading by supercomputers as well as fake swings. This breakout works effectively for many traders.

Position Trading Strategy

One of the long-term currency trading strategies is the position trading strategy. This is the strategy, which does not work in intraday or short term, rather it is for weeks, months, or years on a long-term basis.

For position trading strategy, traders can take positions by looking at the macroeconomic trends of the economies in the long run. The trader can keep his leverage and lot size low as long as he tries to make big profits due to high prices. The Position trading trader needs to have a sound understanding of fundamental analysis and most importantly, he has to be patient as well as have more capital to trade as this strategy does not give immediate profit to many people.

Traders should do fundamental analysis and look for macroeconomic trends. They must then use technical indicators to determine entry and exit conditions and then wait for a favourable outcome, which can take months or years.

Therefore, the position trader should have a thorough understanding of the fundamentals. However, position trading is also beneficial because it does not cause daily stress due to its low-price volatility and is less risky and more rewarding in the long run.

Summary

1. Whatever the business, there is no guarantee of returns and there is also the risk of loss in the business. Therefore, even though the risk in currency trading is low, yet there is a risk of loss as it is a trading in the form of futures and options.

2. For making arbitrage in currency using the calendar spread method, keep in mind that there should be a difference of at least 0.25 points in the price.

3. In currency, you get a lot with very little margin, i.e., around ₹ 2,000. Therefore, a profit of ₹ 200 in this is also 10 percent profit, which is not less. So, don't be tempted to make a profit of more than ₹ 200.

4. Low margin in this does not mean that you should buy 10 lots at once. This is how small investors usually fail. If you have more margin then instead of taking 10 lots of the same currency, you should take 1 lot each of different currency pairs. Then your overall chances of earning will be higher.

5. The period of decline in the currency market lasts long because the economy of a country is determined by the price of the currency and the improvement in the economy cannot occur in a day. So, if you want to become an expert in currency trade, then study the comparative fall and comparative rise of all the currencies. In the currency which comparatively shows the highest growth, make a long deal means buy in the paper and short means to sell in the currency which is comparatively weak.

6. Even though weekly futures contacts are available in the currency it is wise to take at least one month's expiry contact so that you have enough time.

Currency Trading in the Cash Market: In the year 2022 when this book was being written, currency trading was available only in futures and options and not in the cash market. But RBI has announced the launch of digital currency (Digital Rupee). Other countries of the world, the USA, etc., are also going to bring their own digital currency.

If this happens, then you will be able to hold digital currency like shares in your Demat account and buy and sell digital currencies of different countries.

When this happens, you will be able to buy and sell currencies of different countries like shares in the cash market and then ETFs will also be launched in them.

Therefore, the future of currency trading is full of expectations.

❑

20
Be a Smart Investor

"If someone is sitting under the shade of a tree today, it is because someone has planted that tree a long time ago."

–Warren Buffett

Investing from your income is as important as allocating money for monthly groceries, entertainment, petrol, bills, etc. A portion of your income should be regularly invested in investment products that you understand and which can give you a reasonable return on time. As I have always been telling my followers that no matter how little you earn, if you make a strict rule of saving 10 percent of that income regularly, then no power in the world will stop you from becoming rich in the future.

Most people do this too and invest in multiple segments. But very few people become smart investors and for those who become smart investors, their money works and earns for them. This group of people is not necessarily financial experts or gurus, rather they follow some basic rules of investing that make them stand out from the crowd. I will give you a practical example to inspire you—recently I hired an unemployed young man for a part-time job to help me type my books and help with my YouTube blog, etc. I pay him ₹ 6,000 to 7,000 per month. But by working for me and listening to me, he learned to save ₹ 600 per month. He runs his expenses with only ₹ 5400. After learning from me, he got the

Demat account opened. Due to a lower amount, he did SIP in an index fund based on Nifty 50, and in the last 2 years, he has added a fund of about ₹ 15,000 in this way. He is excited about his future and says that if he gets a regular job in the future, he will be able to grow this fund even more rapidly. So, don't make excuses for low income. Your situation cannot be worse than the one I have given as an example.

How to Become a Smart Investor?

There is no exact science to being a smart investor. All you have to do is follow some of the well-known investment methods like saving regularly and investing savings in Equities, SIPs besides commodity ETFs like Gold and Silver and REITs and INVITs of Real Estate. Let me give the example of my wife—my wife regularly does SIP in 3 REITs and 3 INVITs listed in India. Due to this, she is gradually being exposed to real estate and she also gets regular income from them.

Know Your Investment Needs

You must know exactly why you are investing. What are you going to do with these investments once they mature? How much do you need? When do you want it? You need to be clear about how your investments are going to be used in the future. Is it for your child's education, marriage, vacation planning, retirement, buying a home or anything else?

Different people have different aspirations and money is essential, which is clearly needed at different stages of life. So, if you put your invested money in an investment plan today, then you must have a vision for its future use.

Selection of Investment Products

The Indian stock market is one of the most interesting and dynamic places in the world market today. There is a wide variety of investment products available depending on your requirement, such as Mutual Funds, Equity Shares, products like PPF (Public Provident Fund), Gold ETFs, Bonds, Mudra etc.

You should have some basic understanding of the investment product that you choose for your capital and you should invest a small amount in all these products. Often when the market is in a bull run, people do not invest in gold and silver etc. They also ignore PPF, bonds etc. as they are giving low returns. But according to me, it is very important for you to invest in all of them.

Understanding the Level of Risk

Different people have different risk levels. Some invest during a down market and exit as soon as they see a small downside divergence. Some people invest when they enter the market. It all depends on the base of your investment.

If you have done a detailed fundamental analysis of investment options, invested your capital, and are aware of the market conditions, then there is no need to panic. You can stay in the market even if there are minor downsides.

Different investment products carry similar risk levels. For example, there is less risk in the industry with fixed deposits, while equities have relatively higher risks associated with it. This also means that while fixed deposits give you an average return, equities provide good returns.

Diversification of Investments

You must have heard—'Don't put all your eggs in one basket.' Have you tried to employ or translate this proverb into reality?

In fact, it is creditable that you are already investing or thinking of doing so. But you have to make sure that you don't put a major part of your investment capital in one or two investment products.

This diversification of fund allocation can directly help you mitigate your risks and face adverse situations. You have a few fallback options, which can neutralize your damage.

Invest Consistently

One of the most important factors for standing out as a smart investor is to build a habit of investing. Whenever you have extra money, put it to work, invest it. Your regular habit can do wonders and help you stand out from other fellow investors and become a smart investor.

Also, don't worry about how small or negligible the amount is. Even if you invest with a small amount of money, after some time the overall investment value will be good. For example, I advised a newly hired clerk in my office to do a SIP of only ₹ 100 per month. This reduced his fear. After that, I explained to him to put an additional ₹ 10 per month in it and the amount of SIP increased every month. It started becoming 110, 120, 130, 140 per month, which was not much. After a year, this amount became to 220 per month. Every year he also gets an increment, his dearness allowance also increases. That's why his fund increases even after this journey which started from ₹ 100 a month and he expresses his gratitude to me.

Don't Follow Others

You will certainly find self-proclaimed financial gurus, stock market experts everywhere in the investment world. Keep your eyes and ears open and be alert to the happenings in the financial space. This will give you the advantage that you will always be aware of the market dynamics. For example, if you invest in the stock market, you can get suggestions and recommendations from your friends, relatives, stockbroking houses or experts from advisory services and many more.

At the end of every day, you need to do your technical or fundamental analysis to be sure about where you are putting your money.

Educate Yourself

Regardless of whether you are 20 or 50 years old, whether you are an MBA or a student, you need to constantly broaden your horizons and learn to get returns from your investments. For this, you will be required to start from the basics, where you understand the fundamentals to reach advanced investment levels.

But one thing is important – you have to continuously learn and make it a part of your life. There are several ways to do this:

- Read investment books.
- Read investment magazines.
- Subscribe to the financial blog.
- Read financial newspapers.

Portfolio Monitoring

Monitoring your portfolio after a certain period gives you an idea of your return trend. Simultaneously, it also warns you of any potential losses within a specific segment. Keeping these caveats in mind, you can choose to invest based on your risk level, market conditions and high capital.

Investing In Reality

Intelligent and prudent investors do not invest solely on the basis of experience or instincts. Reality is essential in investing. Buying when there is an atmosphere of gloom and selling when there is hope is the main principle of value investing.

Safety Armour

Analysis is essential for investing. But a good investment is the one in which the emphasis is also on safety. Apart from this, all investments are speculative. That's why I always insist on making small profit bookings by buying with cash instead of intraday futures options.

Don't Be Afraid of Instability

The market is always volatile in the short term. So, do not panic and sell your investment when there is a downtrend.

Patience and Perseverance

Investing doesn't mean that you become a winner by beating others. This game is about patience and perseverance. The important thing is how you manage yourself and make yourself a winner.

Don't Repeat Mistakes

If you make making the same mistake repeatedly, then avoid it; use discretion. In the end, the person who earns the money will be the winner.

Don't Copy Others

It is wrong to look at share prices again and again after investing. Selling or buying a stock immediately upon seeing a fall or rise can cause a loss to the investors. If you can't hold a stock for 10 years, don't even think about holding it for 10 minutes. Do not invest money in the market by looking at others. Invest only when you have an understanding of it.

Always Earn Profit

When other people get greedy in the market, then you should become afraid. Be greedy when others are afraid. Always keep such capable managers with you whose interests match yours. Make an investment that is for life, which will always give you profit.

Long Term

If you want the shade of the tree, then you will have to plant that tree years in advance, i.e., invest only after thinking for the long term. Instead of becoming a trader for a day, enter the market with a long-term goal. Wait until the goal is reached. Money grows only by being patient.

Ignore Rumours

Do not invest money in the market by looking at others. Invest only when you have an understanding of it. Ignore rumours. Rumours are rampant in the stock market. It would be better to invest if the shares of a highly regarded or prestigious company are at a fair price rather than buying the shares of a fair company at a higher price.

Keep An Eye on Opportunities

A quick fall in the stock of a reputable company brings a better buying opportunity, whereas most people buy shares when the business of a good company is doing very well. Make an investment for life, which will always give you profit. Always keep an eye out for opportunities that can be found anywhere in the world. Opportunities can exists in any industry.

❑

Conclusion

You have read this book. I am sure that after reading this book which was written with tireless efforts for 7 months, you must have got enough knowledge about investing in Stock Market, Commodity Market, Forex Trading, Mutual Funds etc. to become a smart investor.

The I-5 method, Flow method, Super breakout method, etc. mentioned in this book are the methods discovered by me after years of research. I believe that after reading this book, if you keep investing patiently and slowly according to the stated principles, then no one can stop you from becoming a smart investor.

After reading the book, if you feel that my hard work has been successful and this book has helped you to improve your financial life, then give a 5-star review to this book as a Guru-Dakshina because I am very happy to see your review. Also, your review will encourage other readers and they will also be able to achieve success in their financial life.

Overall, the stock market and investment sector demand from you regular profit booking with patience, in a phased manner, regular investments and without greed. Trading is an art. Its skill can be developed only with practice.

Once you have developed your investment skills, you will be able to easily identify the right time to invest and book profits.

I express my gratitude to the Supreme Lord, the creator of the universe, who made me a medium for writing this book. I pray to that Supreme Being (by whatever name you know him), that Master, that Formless Being, and that Atmantattva to help the readers of this book to understand the principles laid down in this book and achieve financial prosperity through them.

Thank you.

Mahesh Chandra Kaushik
SEBI Registered Research Analyst
Pindwada, District – Sirohi, Rajasthan

❑